Changing Male Roles in Today's World

Richard P. Olson

A Christian Perspective for Men –

and the Women Who Care About Them

Judson Press ® Valley Forge

CHANGING MALE ROLES IN TODAY'S WORLD

Copyright © 1982
Judson Press, Valley Forge, PA 19481

Unless otherwise indicated, the Scripture quotations in this publication are from the Revised Standard Version of the Bible copyrighted 1946, 1952 © 1971, 1973 by the Division of Christian Education of the National Council of the Churches of Christ in the U.S.A., and used by permission.

Also quoted in this book:
    The Bible: A New Translation by James Moffatt. Copyright 1954 by James
    Moffatt. Reprinted by permission of Harper & Row, Publishers, Inc.

Portions from *Green Paradise Lost* by Elizabeth Dodson Gray. Copyright © 1979 by Elizabeth Dodson Gray under its title in the first printing, *Why the Green Nigger?* Reprinted by permission of the author.

Library of Congress Cataloging in Publication Data

Olson, Richard P.
    Changing male roles in today's world.

    Includes bibliographical references.
    1. Men—Psychology. 2. Masculinity (Psychology)
3. Sex role. 4. Men—Religious life. I. Title.
HQ1090.043   305.3   81-23661
ISBN 0-8170-0946-9   AACR2

Because of their part in its conception and creation,
this book is dedicated to
Wally, Dick, Hugh, Ray, Dennis, Arthur, Charlie, Wayne, Buel,
John, Vince, Jim, Dave, Ed, and Jerry, a group of men from
First Christian and First Baptist Churches of Boulder, Colorado.
For several weeks we struggled with these issues. Sometimes
our conversation was awkward and strained,
sometimes it was humorous and joyous, but always it had
integrity and hope; and to
my feminist friends—especially Valerie and Ginny—who
informed me generously, criticized me helpfully, and broke open
aspects of this subject that would never have
occurred to me.

Contents

1

The Way It Was

A Personal, Cultural, Historical Perspective

There is an old folk saying to the effect that "the fish will be the last to discover the ocean." That's how it is with all of us. Many of the things that influence us most are invisible to us because they are so much a part of us.

Just as the fish may be the last to discover the ocean, so we are the last to discover the *culture* in which we live—the way we believe, what we value, how we act and relate to one another, how we do things. Our ways are so familiar to us that they appear to us to be instinctive, or natural, or universal. But this is not so. A little reading or a little travel reveals to us that other people have cultures which are quite different than ours.

One aspect of our culture involves the roles we play. Together we are going to explore men's roles, giving our greatest attention to the ways in which these roles are changing.

But before we do that, let's pause for a moment to discuss the concept of role. Social scientists borrowed the term "role" from the theater; the "role" an actor plays is his or her part. The actor is expected to have certain mannerisms, characteristics, and accent. He or she says certain things and does certain things in given situations because the playwright has created certain expectations for the character being portrayed—the role.

Similarly, the social scientist's definition of a role is: "any pattern of behaviors which a given individual in a specific . . . situation is both: (1) expected and (2) encouraged and/or trained to perform."[1] Or to put it more simply, a role is what is expected of you, both by yourself

7

and by others. You may or may not be aware of these expectations (roles), but they are real.

One of the most important "roles" or set of expectations that exists is our understanding of what it means to be a man or woman, boy or girl. Indeed Deborah David and Robert Brannon have suggested that the roles of male and female (particularly the male role) have influenced and molded our world and social structure more profoundly than any other influence.[2] If that statement seems incredible to you, read on.

A Personal Perspective

I can well remember the first time I was aware of being introduced to male/female roles. (Though, of course, I didn't know those terms at the time.) I was a small child; I don't remember the exact age, but certainly I was preschool. Some older person—I think one of my aunts—quoted to me the first verse of a little poem:

> What are little girls made of, made of?
> What are little girls made of?
> Sugar and spice and everything nice,
> That's what little girls are made of.

Wanting equal time (and playing the perfect straight man), I demanded to know, "What are little boys made of?" And my aunt recited to me the second verse of the poem.

> What are little boys made of, made of?
> What are little boys made of?
> Snakes and snails and puppy dog tails,
> That's what little boys are made of.

I can still recall my childish reaction: "Yuk!!!" Even then, that poem felt like a gyp. I knew I didn't like what it said about me. If I'd thought, I'd have noticed it didn't fit the "little girls" who were my friends either. But there they were in children's verse—stereotypes that influence our understanding of being male, being female.

Shortly after that, I can recall wanting a doll. My sister and her friends seemed to have so much fun playing with dolls, cuddling them, holding them, caring for them, that I wanted one, too. I don't know what feelings my request caused in my parents. Eventually I was given a doll, but not a soft, cuddly one. My doll was a cow*boy,* complete with jeans, denim shirt, and cowboy hat. He was hard and rigid, impossible to hold and cuddle.

I didn't get my cuddly little "doll" until I was twenty-five, and then the "doll" was a real live baby daughter. With what clumsy, awkward, fumbling delight I rocked her, played with her, fed her, changed her!

I couldn't get enough of all those tender experiences with her. I seemed to learn fast, but I still wonder why our society teaches us boys and men so little about the all-important role of father. We ignore the father role in play, an important learning activity. We seem to ignore the father role in other areas of our culture as well.

As time went on, I found myself doing many activities I really didn't want to do but felt somehow forced to do because boys or men did them. I recall I did not like football and was not good at it at all, but I continued to play because somehow I felt that young men should. I remember the taunts one apparently strong teenage boy underwent. He had a heart murmur and was not allowed to play football. The ribbing he took implied that his not playing football was a black mark against his masculinity. However, I almost envied him because at least he had a reason for not playing.

After graduation from high school I left for a small liberal arts college. On the first day there, an acquaintance urged me to go out for football. When I resisted, he invited me down to the locker room to "meet the guys." When we got to the locker room, he—no kidding— stood behind me with both hands on my back, and hollered, "I've got another one. Give him some equipment." They were that hard up for players!

Somehow it seemed my duty to play on that football team. As an eighteen-year-old young man, I was simply unable to face that roomful of guys my age and older and say, "I don't want to play." During that season I sustained an injury that I carry to this day, playing a sport at which I was very poor and which I did not enjoy—but about which I was afraid to say, "I don't like it; no thanks."

I can remember not caring much for hunting even though I grew up in South Dakota, which then made claims of being the pheasant capital of the world! I vividly remember one year when I was invited to go hunting with my new fiance's relatives on opening day. I was unac- customed to the gun which they lent me; in fact, I was afraid of it, and I was not at all interested in shooting pheasants. I only hoped I didn't shoot a future relative! But somehow, hunting was what men did, and so I did it.

What do you remember, and what do you observe about male roles?

Ever wonder why—boys hold doors for girls? women cry and men get angry? men usually drive? many women wear makeup and most men don't? women wear brighter clothes than men and use perfumes entitled Sweet Honesty, while men will not use a scent unless it has a title such as Command, Tackle, or Brut?

These examples and more point to the differences in male and female roles in our cultures. But aren't male and female roles the same every-where? Not at all.

A Cross-Cultural Perspective

One of the most amazing studies of sex roles was done years ago by Margaret Mead when she studied sex roles in New Guinea. Her book about this study is entitled *Sex and Temperament in Three Primitive Societies.*[3]

In the mountains of New Guinea she found "Tribe A." In this tribe both the males and females tend to be mild-mannered, gentle, coop-erative people. They are concerned mostly with nurturing their children, animals and crops. In this tribe it is said that the father as well as the mother "bear a child." Further, these people believe that only the continual caring and involvement of the father can make a child grow in the mother's womb. The father's care is needed also to help the infant continue to grow to healthy childhood. The role of leader or authority figure is undesirable to both men and women. And so leaders are specifically selected in childhood and trained for that role. Otherwise the leadership positions might go begging in that tribe.

Less than eighty miles from this passive, peace-loving tribe, Mead found "Tribe B." In this tribe the ideal for both males and females is to be ruthless, belligerent, and aggressive. Of this tribe she notes "Both men and women are expected to be violent, competitive, aggressively sexed, jealous, and ready to see and avenge insult, delighting in display, in action, in fighting."[4] The entire social order of this tribe is pervaded with hostility, aggressiveness, violence, competition. Children are weaned of parental dependence early and abruptly.

There was a third tribe in this area of New Guinea. We will call it "Tribe C." In this tribe men are expected to be sensitive, emotionally dependent, less responsible, artistic, nervous, gossipy, fond of adorn-ment. The male has "delicately arranged curls, . . . mincing step and self-conscious mein." He lives

"mainly for art and sees the world as an audience for his flute-playing, dancing, carving, and skill at creating costumes. In contrast, the females in this tribe are energetic, impersonal, dominant, practical, efficient. They run all of the important economic and domestic institutions. Females are the sexual aggressors in this society, and the males are less interested in sex, much more passive about it."[5]

Mead notes that in Tribe A both men and women follow roles that we in the United States would traditionally describe as feminine. In Tribe B both men and women have typically masculine roles. In Tribe C the men have our culture's traditionally feminine roles. She concludes:

Many, if not all, of the personality traits which we have called masculine or feminine are as lightly linked to sex as are the clothing, the manners, and the form of head-dress that a society at a given period assigns to either sex . . . the evidence is overwhelming in favor of social conditioning.[6]

Other cultures offer still other illustrations of her conclusion. In Iran men are expected to be emotional while women remain practical and cool. Among the Tutsi of Africa, women are considered physically stronger. In the Navaho and Hopi Indian tribes, one discovers that one tribe considers weaving to be men's work while only women can make pottery; the other tribe believes that the reverse is "natural."[7]

Lack of uniformity of sex roles in different cultures may be clearly seen in still other areas:

Who should always carry the heavy burdens? Men carry them in 12 societies, women in 57 societies.

Who should do the cooking? In 158 societies women are the cooks, while cooking is exclusively a man's task in 5 societies.

Who should manufacture and repair the clothing? Women do this in 95 societies, men in 12 societies.

Who should build the houses? Women do so in 14 societies, men in 86 other societies.[8]

Until recently, some occupations have been viewed by our culture as largely, or solely, the man's domain (the few women in these occupations were notable exceptions). Such occupations included doctor, judge, politician, crane operator. However, the following statistics seem to prove otherwise:

—in Sweden, 75 percent of the crane operators are women.

—in Rumania, over 40,000 women hold political office.

—in Czechoslovakia, 70 percent of the judges at the district level are women.[9]

Traditionally in our society the man has earned the living and the woman has stayed at home and cared for the children. However, on the Cheju island off the coast of Korea, men stay at home and care for the children while the women go out and earn the living. This population of 60,000 has lived in virtual isolation on their island until recently. Before the invasion of tourists, both women and men of Chejo island were quite contented with their work structure.[10]

A Historical Perspective

As we take a quick look at different cultures, we find little that is uniform in men's and women's roles. How, then, did the roles in our culture come to be what they are? Peter Stearns has traced the development of men's roles through the recent changes in Western history. Let us summarize a few of the things he discovered.

Stearns suggests that when discussing male and female roles, one must start with the biological differences between male and female; he suggests that though there is little about man that is biologically determined, "that 'little' is vitally important."[11] Human males are biologically larger and physically stronger (at least in physical force) than women, possess a different hormonal balance than women, and are composed of cells containing a "y" in addition to an "x" chromosome. Stearns argues that it is noticeable from infancy that "men are naturally more aggressive, raucous . . . violent."[12] (This is an item about which there is considerable debate.) Looking back to our biological roots, he notes that the male of the species seems designed not only to provide the sperm, but also to be large enough to frighten away and, if necessary, fight enemies to establish space for breeding and residential purposes. From studying the biology of male and female in our search for male roles we learn that: "It [biology] predisposes, forms a vital background, but does not predetermine effect."[13]

Stearns suggests that to understand present male roles in the light of all our history, we need to add a fourfold overlay on the biological base. The four overlays would be: (a) the implications of any organized society for "manhood"; (b) the ways Western (European and North American) historical/cultural experiences have made their unique imprint on Western males; (c) the challenges and changes that came to maleness from the industrial way of life; (d) the contemporary search for greater flexibility in describing maleness.[14]

Stearns notes that the earliest tradition affecting the role of the man even today is that of the hunting age. In primitive societies women had the task of gathering the vegetable/berry/fruit part of the diet while men had the task of gathering the meat. To be a good hunter, a man needed to be hard, self-sufficient, aggressive, and courageous. He also needed to be able to group together with other males since a man could rarely be successful as a lone hunter.

There was a constant tension among men who were rivals for leadership. Closeness, intricate cooperation, and intense competition all were part of the hunter's life.

Because each hunter needed to be dependable for his task in the hunt, another tradition of manhood was instituted—initiation into manhood from childhood. At a given time the child becoming a man would be tested to see if he had physical courage and self-discipline and if he could withstand pain.

Quite possibly some themes survive from the hunting era: the close association between masculinity and hunting in many persons' thinking; the expectation that aggression and violence may be part of "being a man''; and the custom of ''initiating'' or ''hazing'' young males to see if they have ''what it takes.''

Eventually the hunting society yielded to the agricultural society. One of the new factors in agricultural society was the need to possess a given territory. ''Maleness and property are naturally—some might say tragically—intertwined in agricultural societies.''[15] The property was held by the eldest male, the patriarch. His sons and their families would work for him, awaiting the time when they would inherit the land and the status and leadership that went with it. Stearns notes that at least 30 percent of the males never arrived at that status and had to spend their lifetimes working as hired help for some relative since they were never able to obtain property. (Such a male had no prospect of marriage as well.) Other males, who had the prospect of inheriting property, nevertheless had to wait until their fathers died before it was passed on to them. The ownership and control of property provided status, but this ownership was very unequally distributed indeed.

Within agricultural society, the roles available to men included ''priests, warriors, and farmers.'' And of course most men were farmers. In the work of farmer, the tasks of male and female were not clearly differentiated, although the male's tasks may have had him traveling far from home and performing skills such as butchering, which involved strength and a certain bloodiness. He also maintained prime responsibility for the economic survival of the household.[16] One other aspect of agricultural society we should note. ''Manliness required that nature be viewed as something to be conquered, not appreciated or upheld in superstitious awe. Nature was not a friend. Nature was not beautiful. Aesthetic values have combined only uneasily with manhood in Western culture.''[17]

Some men still live the agricultural style of life, although this number is shrinking each year. But even for those who long ago left the farm, some aspects from this agricultural era have affected our understanding of maleness: the desirability of owning property; the seeming need to protect our own ''territory''; the desire to grow something, even a small garden; and the view of nature as something to be dominated, rather than something with which to live in harmony.

The eighteenth and nineteenth centuries brought the challenge of industrialization, which had profound impact on men's roles. The family became less important as the economic producing unit. Husband, wife, and children no longer worked in partnership to produce their own goods when the work of producing was removed from the home. Decreased infant mortality rates and increased awareness of the importance of child rearing led to an emphasis on man as breadwinner and woman as mother/homemaker. With the rising population, more and more persons became property-less, and therefore, the patriarchal foundation of the society was severely affected and diminished.

Since there was no promise of property, men were much less likely to reside close to their fathers, and as a result extended family ties were weakened. How did the industrial male know he was a man? "The breadwinner role was the classic male obligation in the working class . . . many workers clung to an association of manhood and skill (plus strength of course)." [18] Fathers, lacking the power that went with the promised inheritance of property, began to lose their influence with their sons. Stearns notes a deterioration of relationships between fathers and sons from 1750 onward, reaching its peak about 1900. "Too many fathers were asserting authority that they no longer really possessed. Too many sons could blame their fathers for providing inadequate patrimony. . . ." [19]

For a time the father's authority and leadership influenced the son's choice of work. Until 1900 up to 95 percent of all miners' sons entered their fathers' line of work. Nearly as large a percentage followed their fathers in other fields. In time, however, the influence of the absentee working father diminished. Much smaller numbers of men followed their father's example in work. From the mid-nineteenth century on, as educational opportunities increased, the sons were apt to be better educated and have more occupational choices than their fathers. As a result, a father's influence on his sons and his availability as tutor, guide, and mentor to his sons decreased considerably.

Stearns notes that the industrial revolution had a different impact on the working-class man than on the middle-class man. The young working-class male had real dilemmas about his manhood because the meaning of manhood was not the same as it had been in earlier societies. "Economically dependent, young workers cast about for ways to assert their manhood. The ultimate dilemma was that they never really could. They might leave home, set up their own household and boss it in turn, have their own sons to order around, but they could rarely aspire to property or to the power to make independent decisions." [20] How did the young working-class male deal with this dilemma? "A vigorous subculture developed among working-class male youth, designed to prove masculinity through fighting, wenching, and sometimes drinking. ('When I was eighteen I knew it took four things to be a man; fight, work, screw and booze.')" [21]

In time the work component of that male role became more and more troublesome for the working-class man. Industrial engineers "specifically attempted to eliminate thought, for thought meant delay; workers should become creatures of endless, repeated motion."[22] In this work setting the working-class male quite logically looked for shorter hours and better benefits. His work ceased to have value in and of itself and was seen as having simply instrumental value for nonwork rewards—mainly pay and benefits.

Leisure activities instead of work provided an increasingly important outlet for males. Working-class men developed a male-based recreational pattern of which the tavern was an important part. Vigorous male sports gave them the opportunity to express the physical prowess and skill denied them in their unskilled labor jobs. Personal and family leisure both became important to men. "Belgian miners arguing for a five-day work week around 1908 insisted that they needed one day for sports and drinking and a second day with the family, to recover."[23]

The middle-class male in the industrial era wrestled with somewhat different issues. Though he might have had more authority or power than his working-class counterpart, he engaged even less in the activities associated with maleness—activities requiring personal physical strength, vigorous activity, or high artisan's skills. How could he assert his manliness? Were purely mental and/or clerical and/or managerial activities "manly"? He responded by interpreting his new role in terms of some older male roles.

The middle-class businessman became the new warrior, the new hunter. "Business was hailed as the modern substitute for war, with none of the bloodshed and devastation (only rising prosperity) but with all of the male virtues. . . . Business as battle, the business world as the jungle, corresponded to what men saw around them. . . . A man had to be aggressive to stay afloat. The business mentality produced campaigns, fights, victories, and bitter defeats."[24] Those who were raised, trained, and initiated into this point of view were raised to be "suspicious individualists." Such men found it difficult to form bonds with other males because they were potential competitors. Thus, the aggressiveness of the hunter of an earlier era was called forth, but the hunter's cooperative bonding with others was not.

While much more could be shared, this brief cross-cultural and historical overview may prepare us to consider the issues raised in the following chapter.

2

The Way It Is

A Summary View of Men's Roles Today

Before we are ready to consider men's *changing* roles, we need to become aware of men's *existing* roles. We grew up in a society that had many assumptions about what males should be. These assumptions were so widespread and unquestioned that they were invisible to us. But they were there, and they were all the more powerful because they were unseen.

So let's try to make these unseen assumptions about males visible to ourselves. In our society what is a male supposed to be? How is he supposed to act? What should he always do? What should he never do?

In the drama of our society, what roles are men expected to play? What roles do we expect of ourselves? Let's take a look at how several sociologists describe what they think the role of a man is. Perhaps one of these descriptions will create a spark of recognition in you.

Cowboy or Playboy?

Jack Balswick, University of Georgia sociologist, has suggested that, *"men fall basically into two categories: the cowboy and the playboy."* [1] The cowboy (the John Wayne type) is more at home with animals than with people. He may do things for a person and feel deeply for a person, but he rarely expresses the feelings that he has inside. Ironically, what he feels is many times in conflict with his image of what a male is.

In contrast, the playboy is smooth, nonchalant, and outwardly confident. He is never satisfied with the present and is always on the search for something more. Though he seems to express much warmth and feeling openly, he often does not experience the emotions he expresses.

17

He relates to people, particularly to women, with the intention of manipulating or using them.[2] James Bond, the epitome of the playboy, "plays it cool." He is detached; he does not have deep feelings for those women with whom he interacts.

The cowboy feels, but does not express; the playboy expresses, but does not feel. The cowboy cares, but does not relate; the playboy relates, but does not care. Do you identify closely with either the cowboy or the playboy image? If so, does it feel complete to you?

Is this analysis too simple? Perhaps a more comprehensive view is needed. Deborah S. David and Robert Brannon provide a broader view of the male sex role in their book *The Forty-Nine Percent Majority*.[3]

Four Themes in Maleness

There is no single model of what it means to be a male in our society. David and Brannon note four general themes that in their opinion define the male sex role.

The first theme they point out is *"No Sissy Stuff."* For males, there is a stigma attached to anything that seems even remotely feminine. This stigma applies to every aspect of a man's life and dictates many negative messages.

Don't smell like a woman. Buy deodorant or cologne only if it has a name like Command, Tackle, or Brut. Incidentally, did you know that the scent, English Leather, was originally a woman's cologne until it was renamed?

Don't choose "typical" women's vocabulary, foods, or occupations.

Don't engage in "women's hobbies" such as knitting, flower arranging, doing needlepoint. A 230-pound professional football player who revealed to an incredulous reporter that he liked to do needlepoint was asked, "Aren't you afraid people will think you're a sissy?"

Don't admit to loving art, poetry, music, fine arts, dance (even though ballet dancers train harder and are in better condition than many football players).

Don't be open, vulnerable; above all, don't cry.

Don't reveal your intimate thoughts, values, searchings, uncertainties.

Don't express affection to other males. When you meet an old male friend, don't hug him, but rather hit him on the arm.[4]

The second theme David and Brannon mention is *"The Big Wheel."* Men have a need for success, status; they need to be looked up to or admired by somebody. Be a success! Ordinarily success is defined in terms of money, fame, power, prestige.[5] Usually these fit together. However, extremely high achievement in one area usually gives a man status enough to cause people to ignore his lack of success in other areas.

Since few men will achieve "success" by these standards, they look for alternate ways to be a success. Perhaps they will display symbols of success in the things they buy (for example, cars or stereos), or they will spend their money lavishly and spread it around conspicuously. They may attempt success by being "best" at something—anything really—champion dart thrower, best athlete, fastest mail sorter, best _____ (you fill in the blank).

Still another attempted road to "success" is to show an air of competence that says, "I don't need any help." One woman notes that if a man is asked a factual question he will give an answer, whether he knows anything about the subject or not. Admission of ignorance does not seem to be "OK" for a man. Men have a hard time admitting there is anything they need to know, any help they need from others. Men wander around grocery stores rather than ask a clerk for the location of an item. Men can be hopelessly lost on the road, but they keep driving, hoping they can find a way to solve their lostness themselves. They ask directions only as a last resort. Men risk their backs carrying heavy burdens that could be balanced much more easily between two people rather than call and ask someone to help them. Men struggle alone with personal problems and anxiety that could be much more easily borne if shared with a friend or a counselor.

If all other avenues of success are closed, men turn to one other way to fulfill the "Big Wheel" image, the breadwinner role. At least, a man thinks, he successfully provides his family with food, clothing, and shelter. And yet one more blow to a man's fragile ego can occur when in inflationary times his wife may say to him, "I guess I'd better go to work, too. We can't make it on your paycheck!"

David and Brannon suggest that the third theme in the male role, closely related to the second, is *"The Sturdy Oak."* The male should have a "manly air of toughness, confidence, and self-reliance."[6] This theme refers to the "style" of a man. He should be confident, unconquerable, and serious. He should be his "own man" and always think for himself. "The Sturdy Oak" is a style in which a man communicates strength, independence, calmness. He is composed and unafraid in the face of pain, danger, and even death. He is one who remains cool under all circumstances.[7]

The man may attempt to express this "Sturdy Oak" image through physical strength or athletic prowess. Or, he may need to show his "toughness" in the office or on the job. For example, a new regional manager may fire fully a fourth of his branch managers without considering their competence. He may well do this to show his supervisors that he is tough enough to handle his new assignment.[8]

Because the feelings of most flesh-and-blood males do not coincide with the "Sturdy Oak" style of life, this role expectation can create much inner strain, and sometimes prompt inappropriate action to keep up the image.

The fourth theme that David and Brannon note in the male role is *"Give 'em Hell!"* This refers to "the aura of aggression, violence and daring."[9] The authors note that there is nothing wrong with being a success, or earning respect, or having confidence and determination. Although it can be oppressive to *have* to be these things, the qualities in themselves are quite acceptable by our usual standards. But this fourth theme is neither wholesome nor constructive. "It is the need to hurt, to conquer, to embarrass, to humble, to outwit, to punish, to defeat, or . . . 'to move against people.'"[10] For men, the term "aggressive" is usually taken to be a compliment. "He is an aggressive businessman, . . . or ball player, or thinker. . . ."

Self-defense is assumed to be some kind of "duty" for every male. Robert Brannon recalls a boyhood experience of hiding from a boy named Bobby who had threatened to "bash my head in if I showed up at the bus stop." And so he didn't show up, but rather walked home from school. "Two decades later I can shut my eyes and see the sidewalk on that miserable walk home, remember the shirt I was wearing. . . . It's hard to believe, and I could claim otherwise, but I still feel ashamed."[11]

The "Give 'em Hell" theme shows up in the desire for reckless adventure and daring. At least some time in life (probably youth or young adult years) it is thought that a man should search for life, experience kicks, know adventure. For the person denied adventure and daring in any other way, the reckless risking of life (one's own and others) may occur in high-powered cars, high-speed chases, perhaps mingled with the additional risk of near overdoses of alcohol or other drugs.

Aggressiveness and sex become interrelated as well. Both males and females in our culture have come to think of male sexual aggressiveness as normal and natural. It is almost expected that men will be the sexual aggressors.[12] Somehow male fantasy feeds on such scenes as Rhett Butler carrying a screaming, kicking Scarlett O'Hara up the spiral staircase in *Gone with the Wind*. The theme is more blatantly repeated in the recent movie *The Postman Always Rings Twice* in which a scene that begins with a rape ends with a highly aroused, satisfied woman. The sad part is that this does not stop in fantasy. A reported rape is committed every 14 minutes in the United States (and authorities suspect that 3 to 10 times as many unreported rapes occur.) Studies show that many of these rapes are committed by persons without noticeable psychological illness, that is by "average" males.[13] Such is the tragic merger of violence and sex.

For the man who seemingly is not violence-prone, the car may offer an outlet for aggression. Impatient honking, a waved fist, or an obscene gesture from the safe distance of a car, when no face-to-face encounter is possible, is fairly common on our streets and highways. Undeniably, aggressiveness and violence are an expected part of the male role.

David and Brannon note how these four themes fit together in the male role:

> All together and in its purest form, the male sex role depicts a rather remarkable creature. This hypothetical man never feels anxious, depressed, or vulnerable, has never known the taste of tears, is devoid of any trace or hint of femininity. He is looked up to by all who know him, is a tower of strength both physically and emotionally, and exudes an unshakable confidence and determination that sets him apart from lesser beings. He's also aggressive, forceful, and daring, a barely controlled volcano of primal force. [14]

Of course, no one fulfills all aspects of this male role or even expects to. Some give up on it. A Woody Allen makes humorous hay by being the "lovable loser" who doesn't make it on male expectations but still wants to be considered "a Man." Some men may be obsessed with this role, and some may try to ignore it, but none of us totally escape it. We all have to come to terms with it, one way or another.

Do these four themes of maleness,
"No Sissy Stuff,"
"The Big Wheel,"
"The Sturdy Oak," and
"Give 'em Hell,"
have a familiar ring to you? Which of these themes do you feel is most expected of you? Were there periods in your life in which any of these expectations were stronger? If so, when? Are the expectations, either from outside or inside, stronger than you wish they were?

Ten Commandments of Masculinity

Warren Farrell has suggested that if the "Moses of masculinity" were to hand down "The Ten Commandments of Masculinity," they might look like this:

> 1. Thou shalt not cry or expose other feelings of emotion, fear, weakness, sympathy, empathy or involvement before thy neighbor.

2. Thou shalt not be vulnerable, but honor and respect the "logical," "practical," or "intellectual"—as thou defines them.
3. Thou shalt not listen, except to find fault.
4. Thou shalt condescend to women in the smallest and biggest of ways.
5. Thou shalt control thy wife's body, and all its relations, occasionally permitting it on top.
6. Thou shalt have no other egos before thee.
7. Thou shalt have no other breadwinners before thee.
8. Thou shalt not be responsible for housework—before anybody.
9. Thou shalt honor and obey the straight and narrow pathway to success: job specialization.
10. Thou shalt have an answer to all problems at all times. And above all: Thou shalt not read *The Liberated Man* [Farrell's book from which this is taken] or commit other forms of introspection.[15]

The White Male System

Ann Wilson Schaef is a therapist who discovered that there is an element in life management that goes beyond the usual subjects explored in therapy. In time she discovered that the additional factor with which people had to deal was what she called the "White Male System." She defines this as the system in which we live, the system in which the power, influence, and dominating viewpoint is held by white males. It has its own myths, beliefs, rituals, and ways of doing things. She feels it would be most freeing if we understood this factor for what it is, a system of beliefs, values, methods that has developed. It is not the ultimate reality and is certainly not the way things necessarily have to be.[16]

She suggests that this "White Male System" is fed, sustained, and justified by four myths, myths that have been around so long that most of us are not even aware of them. The first of these myths is that "the White Male System is the only thing that exists." and that therefore the perceptions of other systems (such as the Female System, or the Black System) are "sick, bad, crazy, stupid, ugly, and incompetent."[17] Therefore, this system lacks what Schaef calls a "theology of differences," any method to deal with varying viewpoints or interpretations. The second myth is that "the White Male System is innately superior." The third is that "the White Male System knows and understands everything." That is, men "should and do know it all . . . . If one is innately superior, then by rights one should be omniscient as well."[18] The fourth myth is that "it is possible to be totally logical, rational, and objective."[19] This system thus leaves a man no opportunity to be anything but rational and objective. It neglects the emotional, the subjective, the intuitional resources a man has within himself. All four of these myths can be summarized in yet another unspoken myth that "it is possible for one to be God.'' [20] In other words, if this system in which males are innately superior, understanding, and knowing, and totally logical, rational, and objective, is the only system that exists, ''then they can be God—at least the way the White Male System defines God.'' [21]

She then adds this caution that may well make us aware of the weakness of this system. She points out that being a deity is not easy. It can be quite dangerous for a man to deny his humanity and fallibility. White males who perceive themselves as godlike suffer from heart attacks, strokes, ulcers, and high blood pressure. ''In the end godhood can kill.'' [22]

The religion of this system is the ''Scientific Method'' which provides methods and procedures which can ''prove'' or ''disprove'' anything within the system. She points out that this scientific method assumes the status of an unquestioned religion. Consideration of the possibility that one might use these methods to support one's own beliefs, biases, or prejudices, rarely occurs. By use of this system as a religion, the White Male System reaches an astonishing conclusion, ''that it is possible to control the Universe.'' [23]

Her purpose in pointing all this out is not to say that this system is all bad, but to point out that it is *a* system, not *the* reality, and that there are other systems that deserve consideration as well.

Signs That All Is Not Well

Whether we accept any of the previous descriptions of the male role or not, there is something we must admit. There are clear signs that all is not well with us males. Our physical and mental health and our social behavior all give evidence that things are not well.

Males do not live as long as females and are more susceptible to disease, suicide, crime, accidents, childhood emotional disorders, alcoholism and drug addiction. [24]

More precisely, as George Gilder points out:

''Men commit over 90 percent of major crimes of violence, 100 percent of the rapes, 95 percent of the burglaries. They comprise 94 percent of our drunken drivers, 70 percent of suicides, 91 percent of offenders against family and children.'' [25]

Gilder also points out that the statistics on single men are even more ominous. Single men comprise from 80 to 90 percent of most categories of social pathology. [26]

This information, well known as it is, tells us clearly that something is wrong. Something for males needs to be changed!

Five Difficult Statements

From the information included in this chapter, I make a discovery. The discovery is this: to the extent that I accept my culture's definition of maleness, I find it very difficult to make certain statements. To the extent that I buy into the male role model described above, I find it impossible (or at least very difficult) to say:

1. I don't know.
2. I made a mistake; I was wrong.
3. I need help.
4. I am afraid. (It is difficult to say I *feel* anything, but to recognize and admit fear probably is the most difficult of all.)
5. I am sorry.

If I cannot say these things, my supposed male "strength" becomes a shell that isolates me from a trustful relationship with any other persons, from the opportunity to learn and grow, and from my deepest and truest self.

To the degree that the above analysis of the male role is true, powerful, and operating in my life, I as a male am bound down, boxed in, uptight! And I must confess that it makes me uncomfortable to admit how strong a hold society's definition of the male role has on me and how difficult I find it to resist society's expectations, even when I really want to!

And yet I see things in my life I don't want, and I catch a glimmer of some new qualities in my life that I do want.

But, to what extent are current male roles a reflection of what the Bible teaches that men should be? And in what way are current male/female roles a denial of the biblical vision? To these questions we now turn.

3

On the Way
to What Will Be

Principles of Bible Interpretation

A s the Christian male ponders the roles which he acts out, a question occurs: what does the Bible say? Does the Bible provide perspective for coping with my male identity in a fast changing world?

Is not the traditional male role (authority figure, head of household, leader, wise one, etc.) a reflection of what the Bible teaches that a man should be? Does the Bible support the status quo or lead a man into some radical new change in his male role? If it guides men toward change, what form should that change take? According to the Bible, how should a man relate to his wife (if he has one)? to his children? to his employees or employers? to other men? to women? to his own spirituality? to the society in which he lives?

Some persons find themselves extremely frustrated in the Christian community. They feel that the Christian faith alternately liberates them and represses them. They hear liberating good news in the gospel. But then from the same Bible they seem to hear repressive teachings about what it means to be a woman or a man. Is this true? Need it be so?

What does the Bible say to us as we ponder our male roles? This is a new subject for our society and for us personally.

We will attempt to answer some of these questions in the following chapters. First, our task is to seek an appropriate approach to the Bible on this subject. Then we will see the general direction that this reading of the Bible leads us.

Principles of Bible Exploration

What then are the principles of Bible interpretation that will aid us in gaining insight for changing male/female role expectations?

I submit that a first principle is this: "One cannot absolutize the culture in which the Bible was written."[1] Virginia Ramey Mollenkott points out that there are aspects of culture in Bible times that we would not think of absolutizing. For example, in Bible times, for the most part, the government was either an absolute monarchy or a military empire. No one had heard of democracy. We quite rightly reject those political or military structures today. Also, in Bible times it was assumed that slavery was an acceptable form of ownership. At most, the Bible offers guidelines that make slavery more humane. We do not absolutize that part of the Bible culture either. Further, large portions of the Bible are written with the assumption of patriarchal leadership; not only a male, but the oldest male presides over the clan or tribe, leads it, and makes decisions for it. We abandoned giving the eldest man in our families decision-making power over the rest of the family centuries ago.

Since the time span from Abraham in Genesis 12 through the early church is approximately eighteen hundred years, and since portions of the Bible were written in a number of geographical settings, the question of the cultural settings in which the Bible was written is much more complex than the preceding paragraph might seem to imply.

What was the range of cultural attitudes toward men and women in the Bible? Mollenkott notes that although the Old Testament does reveal some cultic practices which may distress modern women (such as ritual cleansing after menstruation and childbirth), never in the pages of the Old Testament is actual *contempt* for women taught or demonstrated. However, she notes that by the time of the birth of Jesus several generations of rabbinic commentary and custom had lowered the status of women and led to contempt for them. For example, males were taught to thank God daily that they were indeed male. Boy babies were regarded as a special sign of God's favor. Men were instructed to avoid speaking to women in public because of fear that the woman's voice would be a sexual enticement. Women were not allowed to read from the Torah during prayer services or even to pray aloud at their own table.[2] It was such a culture as this that Jesus counteracted at many points in his ministry. Paul wrestled with this kind of rabbinical training as he dealt with the place of men and women within the grace of Christ. At any rate, our first principle is that we do not absolutize the cultural setting or cultural teachings of any period in which the Bible was written.

The second principle of Bible interpretation emerges from the first. In reading the Bible, one should discern carefully between the cultural assumptions and the explicit teaching of the Bible. According to Mollenkott we need to make delicate and careful distinctions between what is written "for an age" and what is written for all times. To admit that both types of literature may exist side by side within the Bible is to begin to be able to hear a fresh word being spoken there.

Some persons may draw back from this principle, fearful that it suggests that the Bible is not an authority for living. Others may wonder, "Won't such a reading lead to rationalization in which one explains away anything one does not want to obey? Is it not possible that any difficult Bible teaching can be explained away as 'cultural' so that one can do anything he or she wants to?"

If we were to stop with this principle, self-serving rationalization might indeed be a real danger, but we add two more principles of Bible interpretation.

According to the third principle, we begin our study of the Bible by discovering the major Bible themes, doctrines, commands. There is quite general agreement among Bible scholars about what these major Bible themes are:

—God is creator.

—God created male and female in the image of God.

—All of us have fallen short of the glory of God.

—God loves humankind undeservedly and graces us freely in Jesus Christ.

—Each of us is called to make decisions for Christ and thus to become new persons with infinite possibilities (even Christlike).

—In Christ, God gives each of us gifts and fruit of the Spirit which are to be used in service of God.

—Jesus summarized all the commandments by which we are to live in calling us to love the Lord our God with all our heart, soul, mind, and strength, and our neighbors as ourselves.

Others might want to add other Bible themes, doctrines, or commands to this list, but most will agree that the above is a rather basic summary.

Starting with these themes, we reason to the specifics of male and female roles. If the Bible seems to be silent about some issues of the male role that concern us, we can justifiably imply biblical guidance from these themes. When reading a Bible passage and trying to untangle the cultural conditioning and the timeless word, these themes may guide us. Whatever in the Bible passage that is in accordance with these themes is the timeless word; what is not may well be cultural background.

But there is one more principle that gives us even more specific guidance. The life, behavior, and teachings of Jesus Christ provide specific guidance in working on male and female roles. The Christian faith has always affirmed that not only is Jesus God with us, not only is he the one who saves and reconciles the world to God, but he is also the one who lives out a life of obedience to God. He does so in human flesh and in our midst.

Two aspects of Jesus' life speak to us on these matters. First, he is a model of life as God intends it to be. Humanness, the ways males and females relate to each other, how one lives with one's own spirituality, and one's emotions—all of these are modeled in the life of Jesus of Nazareth.

But there is yet another biblical image of Jesus that is instructive at this point. Four times in the Bible, Jesus is described by the Greek term *archēgos*. This term can mean several related things: founder, source, origin. William Barclay suggests "An *archēgos* is some one who begins something in order that others may enter into it. . . . An *archēgos* is one who blazes the trail for others to follow."[3] And so this term can mean author, originator, founder, or leader. Perhaps the most accurate and vivid translation of *archēgos* is "pioneer."

The four references using "pioneer" as the translation of "archegos" are: Acts 3:15 (Moffatt)—"You killed the *pioneer* of life"; Acts 5:31 (Moffatt)—". . . as our *pioneer* and saviour"; Hebrews 2:10—". . . the *pioneer* of their salvation . . ."; Hebrews 12:2—". . . looking to Jesus, the *pioneer* and perfector of our faith."

Jesus, then, is described as pioneer of life, salvation, and faith. In addition to being our model, he is our pioneer.

I find it instructive to think of Jesus both as model and as pioneer. I see him clearly modeling how to listen to the voice of God and be guided by it rather than by a culture that sometimes degrades or dehumanizes human beings, the objects of God's love. His powerful interaction with his culture calls me forth to look at my culture with new eyes. I am intrigued not only by what he modeled but by what he pioneered, by what he began. He began a process, blazed new trails, and started us down those trails. As we move into a radically different culture from the one in which he lived and attempt to follow his pioneering example, we may find ourselves facing new problems, decisions, and directions which receive only the vaguest hints in the pages of the New Testament.

In summary, then, I suggest four principles of Bible interpretation as we attempt to gain insight to deal with modern issues in a fast changing world.

The four principles are: (1) do not absolutize the culture(s) in which the Bible is written; (2) carefully distinguish the cultural assumptions from the explicit teaching of the Bible; (3) reason from major Bible themes, doctrines, commands to the specifics of male and female roles; (4) use the life, teachings, and behavior of Jesus Christ as both model and pioneer to provide specific guidance.

Thus the Bible calls us back to basic beliefs and behavior. The Bible also calls us forward—led by Jesus, the pioneer who goes before us (Mark 16:7) into the new and unknown problems and issues of each age.

Applying the Principles

As a starter, let's apply the principles I've suggested to two questions: (a) what should be our understanding of maleness and femaleness? (b) how should we respond as Christians to the male role as summarized from David and Brannon in the previous chapter?

What do the major Bible passages—doctrines, themes, concepts—say to us about maleness and femaleness?

In the first two chapters of Genesis, there are two vivid images of the creation of man and woman in the two poems of creation that are found there. "God created man in his own image, in the image of God he created him; male and female he created them. And God blessed them, and God said to them, 'Be fruitful and multiply . . . and have dominion . . .'" over the created order (Genesis 1:27-28). Both were created together, both were created in the image of God, both were given dominion over the rest of creation. When we absorb this biblical teaching, we are prepared to accept what our socialization has ignored— that a human male has more in common with a human female than with any other creature. Both the human male and the human female share a special endowment from God and a special possibility of relating to God that creates between them a basis for respect, love, and community.[4]

In the second account of creation (Genesis 2:4-25) woman is created by God from the rib of man (vv. 20-25). Again, the Bible makes very clear that God created woman and man for each other because they alone have the possibility of a very special deep community and spiritual harmony with each other. Man was alone with all the animals and "there was not found a helper fit for him." So God concluded, "It is not good that man should be alone" and created the woman. Mollenkott notes that verses 23-24 contain a pun on Hebrew words for *man* and *woman* to underscore the essential oneness of the human race. "This shall be called woman *(ishshah)* for from man *(ish)* this was taken. This is why a man leaves his father and mother and is united to his wife, and the two become one flesh."[5] Mollenkott notes further that there is no hint of domination by Adam and submission of Eve before they fall into sin. In Genesis 3:14-19, after the fall God describes a number of unpleasant changes that will occur because of their alienation from their God. Among that list of unpleasant consequences is the dominance of men over their wives.[6] This dominance is not a desired condition. It is a tragic consequence of people being out of harmony with God and with each other.

As we move on from the subject of the creation of man and woman in the image of God, we consider the implications of the Christian concept that God loves us undeservedly and graces us in Jesus Christ. While most persons probably assume that this love and grace are for women and men equally, we need to realize how thoroughly male Jewish religion was at the time of Christ and recall the position of contempt that women occupied. Then maybe we are ready to see the shocking, revolutionary way that Jesus included women in his ministry:

He invited women to believe in him. When a woman cried out, "Blessed is the womb that bore you and the breasts that you sucked," he responded, "Blessed rather are those who hear the word of God and keep it" (Luke 11:27). She was saying, "I wish I was your mother so I could relate to you." In essence, he responded, "You don't have to be my mother to relate to me. You can relate to me in direct personal belief."

He talked with women, discussed deep issues with them repeatedly, and even taught in the court of women at the temple so that women could have access to what he had to offer. He saw listening to and conversing with him as most appropriate ways for a woman to relate to him. She didn't have to be in the kitchen (recall the Mary-Martha episode—Luke 10:38-42).

He touched women publicly. For example, he touched and healed a woman who had been a cripple for eighteen years. He touched her and called her a daughter of Abraham, a very special title (Luke 13:10-17).

He allowed women to touch him even when the intimate gestures of love and affection could have embarrassed him publicly (Luke 8:43-44).

He allowed women to support him emotionally and financially. (See, for example, Luke 8:3.) While he chose men to be with him, he also considered the companionship and support of women to be important.

He called forth loyalty from women, and they followed him to the end. Indeed, women were the first to witness the empty tomb, the first to be encountered by the risen Christ.

As Scanzoni and Hardesty summarize effectively:

> Thus Jesus' life on earth from beginning to end outlines a paradigm for women's place. His actions upset and appalled his contemporaries, dumbfounded his critics, and flabbergasted his disciples. Since that day the church has struggled, if sometimes unenthusiastically and unsuccessfully, to cut through the barbed wire of cultural custom and taboo in order to emulate the one who promised both men and women, "If the son makes you free, you will be free indeed!"[7]

This Jesus, who came to all, called each person to decision. Those who chose to follow Christ were given the power to become children of God, were given gifts and fruit of the Spirit, and were entrusted with infinite possibilities.

The new community which was created in Christ Jesus is dazzlingly portrayed by Paul in Galatians 3:28. "There is neither Jew nor Greek, there is neither slave nor free, there is neither male or female; for you are all one in Christ Jesus."

Mollenkott suggests that the meaning of this great passage is not that males and females are going to lose their biological differences. Rather, the Bible passage promises freedom and psychological wholeness fostered by Christian fellowship. Thus, "each male and each female would be free to develop his or her gifts without reference to gender-based stereotypes."[8]

Men and women are called to mature personhood in the image of Christ, to Christlikeness. The Holy Spirit gives to the person of faith (male and female) the fruit of the Spirit that is listed in several New Testament passages. Scanzoni and Hardesty combine and summarize these in the following list of what they refer to as "the best in human qualities: love, joy, peace, patience, kindness, goodness, faithfulness, gentleness, self-control, humility, integrity, meekness, sensitivity, empathy, purity, submissiveness, confidence, courage, strength, zeal, determination, compassion, common sense, generosity, self-sacrifice.

"Against such there should be no law for any person in any culture."[9]

Read that list slowly. Which of these would usually be thought of as masculine qualities, and which are most frequently considered feminine qualities? In the new community that Jesus Christ creates, these gifts are available to all. They are to be claimed by both men and women. If one uses the study principles I have outlined, one can see that the Bible reveals the personhood, potentiality, worth, and relatability of each person—male or female.

But let's move on to one other issue. How do we view the four aspects of the typical male role in our culture as summarized by David and Brannon in the previous chapter? In particular, how do we view them in the light of the modeling and pioneering lifestyle of Jesus of Nazareth?

One aspect that they noted is that males should have "no sissy stuff." There is a stigma attached to "all stereotyped feminine characteristics and qualities, including openness and vulnerability." [10] Jesus quite clearly challenged this because he lived a life of great sensitivity and vulnerability. When he felt the slight touch of an ill woman, a woman afflicted with constant menstrual flow for twelve years, he responded to the touch. Japanese author Shusaku Endo comments, "To me the affecting part is how Jesus felt all the woman's heartbreaking suffering through the touch of her trembling finger against his clothing. . . . The woman's finger reaches furtively from behind other people, and when it barely comes in contact with his outer garment, Jesus turns and understands her suffering." [11]

He was in touch with his feelings and not afraid to show them. His anger was instant, clear, and frightening. He was not ashamed to shed tears over a friend or a city. He was able to relax, play, enjoy a party even in the midst of horrible pressures. And he was free to turn aside from a party to respond to a crying human need.

Having feelings usually associated with women was not threatening to Jesus nor was using feminine images about himself threatening to him. He once wept over a city and longed to gather it as a hen gathers its chicks under its wing. Jesus challenged a "no sissy stuff" life-style again and again.

The second contemporary male role theme noted by Brannon and David is "The Big Wheel: success, status, and the need to be looked up to." [12] Again, Jesus seems to have lived in contrast to this contemporary male role. He once told a zealous, would-be follower that he didn't even have a place to lay his head. Once when his followers were jockeying for positions in what they anticipated would be places of authority in an earthly kingdom, Jesus put a child in their midst and asked them to become as children. Another time, while the struggle for position among his followers continued unabated, he counseled them, ". . . Let the greatest among you become as the youngest, and the leader as one who serves. For which is the greater, one who sits at table, or one who serves? Is it not the one who sits at table? But I am among you as one who serves" (Luke 22:26-27). And another Gospel writer recalls that Jesus demonstrated this by kneeling at his disciples' feet and washing them, one by one. Jesus seemed to be completely free of the need to be "The Big Wheel."

The third theme in contemporary male roles that David and Brannon noted is "The Sturdy Oak," the need to express a "manly air of toughness, confidence, and self reliance."[13] Jesus did not fit this mold either. The Gospels quite explicitly say that he chose twelve "to be with him." He never denied his need for human community and support. He led them into an ever-deeper community and at the climax of his ministry called them "friends." He did not hesitate to express his love for them, to let them touch him, lean upon him, embrace him.

And he was quite transparent about a prayer life that expressed a constant reliance on God for guidance, support, empowerment. Jesus was no "Sturdy Oak." He refused to exist as though he did not need friendship and companionship, both human and divine.

The fourth theme in contemporary male roles defined by David and Brannon was the "Give 'em Hell!" attitude of "aggression, violence, and daring."[14] Jesus seemed to recognize the need for anger and for force on appropriate occasions. The Gospels record his anger at times, and they tell us that at least once he used force. But he was not locked into this style, not by any means. He calmed down disciples who wanted him to call down fire on a village that refused his message. Then, the most violent night of his life, when he was taken to be crucified, one of his disciples swung a sword wildly. Jesus' word to that disciple was, "Put your sword back into its place; for all who take the sword will perish by the sword" (Matthew 26:52). His unfulfilled desire for his contemporaries was, "Would that . . . you knew the things that make for peace!" (Luke 19:42a).

And so by his modeling and pioneering, Jesus challenges much of the contemporary description of what it means to be a man in our culture. And yet we must honestly ask, "Who lives more fully? The person who buys into the themes of contemporary maleness, or the One from Nazareth?"

Following Jesus' example, we are set free from some of the cultural constrictions on our male role. He allows us to challenge some existing assumptions and search for a new way.

Perhaps we are now ready to start talking about some specifics in a new style of life for men. We turn now to look at some of those specifics.

4

Claiming the Freedom to Feel

Emerging Emotions

I still remember the shock of recognition I experienced the first time I read the chapter on men's emotions in Herb Goldberg's *The Hazards of Being Male*.[1] His title of that chapter, "Feelings: The Real Male Terror," seemed to say it all. As I read the chapter, I remember thinking that the difficulties men had with their emotions were not as bad as I thought they were; they were worse!

In my training as a pastoral counselor, I felt that I had had experiences through which I had freed myself to recognize and express my emotions more than many of the males I knew as friends or as counselees. And yet I recognized that there was a cultural bondage on me and my emotions as well, a bondage that was often unseen.

If liberation for men is ever to occur, a most basic aspect of what men will gain will be the freedom to feel. They will claim not only the freedom to feel but also the freedom to express what they feel.

A man's most basic task in the whole liberation struggle is first and foremost to get in touch with himself. The task does not end there, of course, but freer emotional awareness and expression are the beginning of many good things for everybody, especially for those of us who have been taught to deny and suppress our emotions for so long.

When Goldberg was asked what needs or impulses or emotions males are blocking, he answered, *"More or less all of them."*[2]

And so let us take a hard look at ourselves. Our question needs to be not only "What is my experience in regard to my emotions?" but also "What would I like my emotional life to be if things could be different for us men?"

I will share·with you a list of emotions that men either deny or have difficulty expressing. As you read this list, use it to become more conscious about yourself. Ask, "Which emotions on the list are most difficult for me to admit? to feel? to express? to accept in another?"

Incidentally, I shared the following list of emotions with thirteen men in a men's consciousness-raising group which I led. I asked them to check which ones they felt they had difficulty admitting or expressing. Every emotion on the list was checked by at least two men. Many of the emotions on the following list were checked by half to two-thirds of the men in that group. For our group Goldberg's observation that we are blocking more or less all of our emotions was accurate. Take a look for yourself.

The Emotions Denied Us

Dependency and Passivity

From infancy on, a young male child is taught that males should not depend on anybody. Dependency in the male seems to be equated with weakness, and that spells disaster.[3] Even normal dependency needs seem to be suppressed in the lives of many males.

It is considered equally "bad" for a male to be passive, to lean back and do nothing. Boys are taught that boys are supposed to produce, be adventurous, stay in motion, and have unlimited energy. A young male hopes to be a Tom Sawyer balancing himself on the picket fence while an adoring Becky watches and admires him from below. If a boy sits passively in a corner reading a book, his parents fear something is the matter with him.[4]

In adult life, this resistance to dependency and passivity shows up in a number of ways: an obsession with work, the inability to relax, the inability to play except in highly competitive situations, restlessness on weekends, discomfort during vacations, and the inability to retire from the working world gracefully.

It also appears in male resistance to admitting that he is ill, needs a doctor, or needs time to recover from illness or surgery. Goldberg tells the story of a forty-nine-year-old self-made millionaire. This highly successful man learned he needed open heart surgery and underwent a nine-and-a-half-hour operation. Eight days later when his wife picked him up from the hospital, he did not go home but went back to the office to work.[5] Back to work following life-and-death surgery after eight days, because "real men" aren't sick; if they are, they get over it quickly! When you stand outside and look at such an example, does it seem reasonable or realistic? And yet are there similar examples in your life? If this millionaire is an extreme example, how many males to a lesser degree deny illness, postpone getting help, and go back to work much too soon after illness or surgery?

This fear of passivity or dependency appears also in our resistance to sleep. Somehow it seems "manly" not to need sleep, certainly not to need sleep during the daytime.

I must admit that occasionally I undergo this embarrassing humorous scenario: an infrequent emergency call comes in the middle of the night. The caller asks me, "Did I wake you?" I will assure him or her I was awake, although I am at the moment attempting to wake up, trying to get in touch with reality, and obviously lying! We males have a hard time admitting that even in the middle of the night we need to be dependent or passive!

Vulnerability or Asking for Help

Somehow we seem to learn that a major indicator of "manliness" is the ability to say, "I can do it by myself. I don't need any help." "God helps those who help themselves."[6]

In the everyday affairs of life, our difficulty in asking for help merely inconveniences us. It may take us longer to grocery shop, to find the items in the hardware store, to find our way to our destination in a strange city, or to fix the broken item than it would if we had been willing to ask for help.

However, when a man will not reach out to a friend or professional when he is hurting desperately inside, then the inability to say, "Help me," is tragic indeed. When a man cannot cry for help, he suffers and struggles in silence. Eventually he breaks down or perhaps even commits suicide. Frequently even his closest friends are surprised. They didn't know anything was wrong.[7]

Warren Farrell recalls an experience shared in a consciousness-raising group by a man named Larry. Larry and his friend Joyce were riding in Larry's car (Joyce was driving), and unaccustomed to the car's steering mechanism, Joyce swerved the car into oncoming traffic. Several cars narrowly missed them, and a bus stopped within inches of the car. People from the bus piled out to help them. Larry recalls that some women went up to Joyce, inquired if she were upset, talked to her in supportive ways, and encouraged her to cry and thus obtain the needed relief from the tension of the situation. Men from the bus approached an equally shaken Larry, quickly inquired if he was all right, *then asked about the car*. They then discussed the steering mechanism and other mechanical difficulties. When Joyce and Larry returned to their car, it was obvious that Joyce felt relief from the tension of the accident while

Larry still had tremendous tensions pent up within him. "By allowing Joyce to appear weak, society allowed her to gain internal strength, while Larry suffered the consequences of surface strength."[8]

How needlessly we suffer because of the assumptions that we are invulnerable and therefore don't need help!

Sadness and Tears

In childhood boys are quickly told, "Big boys don't cry." When a boy forgets this, he is called "Crybaby." These beliefs resonate within us and block the flow of tears and the full experience of sadness. A twenty-three-year-old patient of Goldberg recalls:

> When I was twelve years old my father mocked me for crying one time. I consciously made a decision right then and there that I would never cry again. . . . When I finally realized crying is good, and that men need to cry too, I couldn't do it any more. Since then I've been trying to learn to cry again, and it's been very difficult. The same thing goes for other feelings. It's very hard for me to let myself experience them most of the time.[9]

He is not alone. Many men once resolved that they would never cry again—a resolution too frequently kept.

It is one of those strange quirks of our culture that a woman's tears call forth a protective attitude from those around her, while a man's tears often occasion discomfort or disgust at his lack of control. A friend of Warren Farrell's told him that at one time he broke down in tears to a colleague at work as a result of frustrations at the office and tragedies in his personal life. He recalls:

> The news of my crying was all over the office in an hour. At first no one said anything. They just sort of looked. They couldn't handle the situation by talking about it. Before this only the girls had cried. One of the guys did joke, "Hear you and Sally been crying lately, eh?" I guess that was a jibe at my masculinity, but the "knowing silence" of the others indicated the same doubts. What really hurt was that two years later, when I was doing very well and being considered for a promotion, the crying incident was brought up again. My manager looking over my evaluations, read a paragraph to himself and said, "What do you think about that crying incident?" You can bet that was the last time I let myself cry.[10]

When I told this story to a men's awareness group, it occasioned much discussion. One man commented that where he worked, even if a man received a word of a death in his family while at work, he would show no outward expression. He certainly would not cry. Another man said that his boss instructed employees, "Leave your emotions at the door when you come to work." I asked the group, "Has anyone here ever cried at work?'' One man responded, ''I've cried about work, but never at work, not even with work colleagues. I longed for that kind of rapport, but it was just never there.''

Personal and societal feelings against men's public expression of their tears seem to run deep.

Sympathy—Empathy—Tenderness—Transparency

Some people frown at a man's tears not only when they are for himself but also when they are shed in behalf of someone else. Sympathy (which literally means ''feeling with another'') and empathy (which literally means ''infeeling'' or ''feeling into another's experience'') are awkward and difficult expressions for many men. One young man told psychologist/author Phyllis Chesler that he felt uncontrollably vulnerable whenever he experienced empathy for the suffering of others. '''It tears me apart. I feel castrated,' he said. 'I'd rather have a group of guys coming at me with knives than feeling this awful feeling.''' [11]

A closely related subject in which there seems to be a clear male pattern is in the lack of ''transparency'' or ''self-disclosure.'' Some years ago Sidney Jourard carried on research that showed that men typically reveal less information about themselves to others than women do. Also, his studies revealed that men receive less personal information from others than women do. This avoidance of being known is (in Jourard's opinion) apt to be a negative factor in a man's mental health. This lack of self-disclosure is apt to lead to less insight into his own needs, less empathy with others, more misunderstanding of other people and their needs, and feeling less meaning and value in his existence. Jourard concludes that lack of self-disclosure causes a man to be out of touch with himself, therefore unable to be in touch with others (in empathy with them), less able to provide for his needs or those around him, and, as a result, more subject to depression and defeat in living. [12] If a man is to escape this trap and find community through sharing his inner life, he must somehow escape that ''Sturdy Oak'' attitude, which our culture seems to call forth in males.

Fear

Goldberg notes that ''words like 'chicken s_____,' 'scaredy cat,' 'coward,' 'gutless,' 'no balls,' and 'sissy' ring in the male's ear a lifetime and often drive him into senseless, self-destructive, even crazy behaviors and risk-taking in order to prove to himself and others . . . that he isn't afraid.'' [13]

In my impression fear is the emotion most difficult to admit or express. It is also the emotion least allowed us by those around us. One woman who was in the process of becoming liberated said of her male companion, "I don't mind if he cries once in a while, but I'd feel very uncomfortable if he were afraid." Another feminist spoke of herself and her husband, "I want to be free to experiment with my assertiveness and power, but I hope George will always be calm and dependable when I need him." If those women mean that they hope those men will *always* be strong, dependable, and fearless, they are laying an impossible heavy burden on them. And the men, being men, will probably accept that burden to the detriment of all.

Sometimes when persons describe to me what my relationship means to them, they say, "Dick, you're a rock." I suppose that means fearless, reliable, enduring. For the most part that feels good. For instance, I still recall with pleasure an experience that occurred years ago. My infant daughter awoke with terror, frightened by a sudden thunderstorm. I lifted her from her crib, brought her to my wife's and my bed. I laid her on top of me, and feeling my absence of fear, she instantaneously fell asleep. I liked being that calm, unfearful person for her, and I still usually like being that same sort of person for others. (Thunderstorms don't frighten me, but some other things do.)

But I, too, am mortal, fragile, and frail in a world that has too many dangers, uncertainties, changes. Please, dear brother or sister, allow me my fear if you want to experience my strength. And allow the same to yourself and those around you.

Fear of Failure

So far we have been speaking of fear in general. There is one fear that is particularly inhibiting, the fear of failure.

As a youth, I worked for a construction contractor who would respond to our mistakes with such words as these: "The man who never makes a mistake never makes anything. Let each mistake be a signpost on the road of your life, but don't go by that same signpost again." Unfortunately, most of us are not as tolerant of mistakes or failure in ourselves or others.

As a late teenager I can recall envying my male friends who boasted that they had never been turned down by any young woman they had asked to go out with them. I could not say that. I'm sure it was nice for them to feel so successful, but now I wonder why it was so important *always to succeed*. The compulsive need to succeed is part of a matched pair; the other half of the pair is the fear of failure.

The fear of failure is a powerful time bomb capable of destroying every man that does not succeed in defusing it. When a man is in its grip, he never discovers what he really wants. All he knows is what he doesn't want. *"He doesn't want to fail."* [14]

When one has a fear of failure, each victory or success is basically hollow and short-lived. The achievement makes failure seem all the more imminent since it raises the standard of success and makes this standard more difficult to achieve.

How much wiser we would be, how much more fully we would live if the fear of failure did not terrorize us so! Failure could then be seen as a message to us that could help us steer a more true course. If a relationship failed, we could learn from it, part friends, and grow from the failure. If we failed in a job, we might find a message that we had been misdirecting our energy and could then go look for new directions for ourselves. We could even learn from illness; it might reveal to us bad habits we needed to correct. [15]

Anger and Aggression, Particularly Anger Toward Women

Though angry aggression is recognized and admitted in men, its expression must be curiously limited. It is expected that one's aggression will be expressed impersonally, toward strangers, competitors, enemies, or other outside targets. In other words, a man is guided to displace his anger/aggression *away from* those with whom he regularly interacts (and probably those who called forth the anger), *toward* those with whom he has very little contact. [16]

In particular, a man discovers that he should not have angry confrontations with a woman. Win or lose, a male is considered a "bully" for fighting with a female. Young or old, a male is taught that the female is fragile, that she needs to be protected, and that she should never be considered his opponent.

This prohibition against expressing anger toward women has particularly tragic consequences. For one thing, it means that males and females who accept this prohibition never relate on an equal basis. Further, this "defense against anger will spell the death of spontaneous sexuality." Further still, the attempt to avoid anger toward the female may cause the male to feel exceedingly guilty toward her since anger is almost certain to emerge from time to time in any intimate relationship. Finally, this prohibition on anger against females many times hastens the death of deep feeling between two people who once had had an intimate relationship, and may contribute to their detachment and withdrawal from each other. [17] As long as a male and female cannot admit, recognize, express, and negotiate their anger with each other, their relationship will be crippled. In a day of increasing feminine consciousness, a woman may be getting in touch with—and expressing— a good deal of anger toward the men in her life. If the men operate by the old rule which says, "Don't be angry with women," the end result can only be frustration and alienation.

But, when this prohibition is broken and the skills of dealing with anger are learned, the possibility of meaningful new depths of relationship await both man and woman. They can learn to live beyond anger, comfortable with their strength to deal with conflict when it emerges.

An equally tragic phenomenon exists when some males direct all of their anger toward females. Perhaps unfortunate early experiences have stirred this anger. Perhaps these men perceive women as having less power and thus attack them as the only people they dare attack. This kind of abuse needs careful help so that it can be stopped. If you find yourself in this circumstance, I urge you to find a good professional counselor or therapist.

Depression

Inevitably the suppression of personal needs, angers, and fears, along with a good-sized dose of personal insecurity will lead a man into times of depression. Life may very well seem overwhelming, the demands and expectations on him too great, the hope for living up to them very dim indeed.

But even this depression is denied the male—or at least any public admission of it. If a man ever admits to depression, he admits it only to someone whom he has chosen as most trustworthy, and he never mentions it outside that intimate partnership.

If he lacks that intimate partner, he probably will not even know what is "bugging him," he will know only that he is losing his edge, slipping in his effectiveness, and not enjoying anything any more.

Miscellaneous Other "Forbidden Emotions"

Goldberg mentions many other emotions that men are blocking from their experience. For one, men do not feel free to be impulsive. Somehow young males get the message that they are "animals" who need to be "tamed" by some woman in marriage. Men are somehow quite fearful of what they would do if they were free to be spontaneously impulsive.

Men are also not permitted "irrational behavior." "Silliness, clowning, being spontaneously playful and even laughing uninhibitedly (rather than controlled snickering) are beyond the comfortable repertoire of typical male expressions." [18] Should a male act in this manner, he is apt to receive pained, embarrassed expressions that wordlessly communicate "You're making a fool of yourself." If his wife is present, she may well try to quiet him down.

Somehow we link being masculine and being logical, analytical, scientific. In so doing we develop a fear of anything not scientifically verifiable or concretely visible. Therefore, we men may lack alternative methods to perceive what is going on, such as intuition, the ability to sense or feel what is happening.[19]

Another male presupposition that needs to be challenged while we are on the subject of male rationality is that emotional expression hampers clear thinking. Warren Farrell raises an important question when he writes, "Must a person who expresses emotions think without logic or does it ultimately free one to think logically?"[20] Emotions color one's thinking whether they are recognized and admitted or not. It is probable that one who is in touch with emotions and expresses them freely may see things most accurately and make decisions most logically and perceptively.

A man also fears ambiguity. This may carry over into a male's relationships. Since few situations or relationships admit to a clear analysis, the male may experience much discomfort around such subjects and avoid them as much as possible.

The Results of Denial of Emotions

Though men are urged to get in touch with their feelings in popular circles today, the male knows that expression of all of his feelings is not acceptable, nor is the expression of any of his feelings acceptable in some arenas where he must move. He has to be particularly careful at places where he has a lot to lose such as at work. Even if a male discovers the freedom to express some of his emotions, he must be careful to do so only when he has discovered that it is acceptable to do so in a certain setting. He is forced to split his emotions. He is allowed to let some feelings come through but only in safe places. It is necessary for him to mask his feelings almost everywhere else.[21]

Goldberg notes a number of destructive consequences for the male who has repressed his emotions.

1. He is vulnerable to sudden, unpredictable behavior. . . .
2. He denies his feelings and needs and then becomes resentful because intimates take him at face value and don't read his hidden self correctly. . . .
3. [He becomes] prone to emotional upsets and disturbances. . . .
4. [He becomes] prone to countless psychophysiological disorders.
5. The defenses against feeling force him further and further away from relationships.
6. His inability to ask for help means that when his defenses do begin to

shatter . . . his only alternative is to withdraw even more or to numb himself with alcohol or drugs.[22]

Perhaps only when inhibitions have been relaxed by a few drinks will he ever admit to the feelings, frustrations, and pain that are inside him.

What Must I Do to Be Whole?

When the men's group of which I was a part discussed emotions, we had a difficult time. Even though the members in the group had developed some trust for each other, we felt extremely uncomfortable even talking *about* emotions, much less expressing those that might be bubbling inside. I asked the men what made it so hard to talk about feelings, and they gave me several answers. One man said he found it hard to recognize that he was feeling anything, much less recognize what the feeling was and the reason for it. Others agreed that they had had years of practice ignoring and denying such impulses. Others said they sometimes were quite aware of an emotion but felt awkward or shy expressing that to someone else. How do we get out of such traps?

First, recognize and admit that this is an area of need in your life. Since you probably don't have problems in all of the areas described in this chapter, you may use the areas in which you do *not* have problems to convince yourself that you don't have any problems at all. But no healing can come unless you recognize that blocking of emotions is occurring in your life. Admit it. What in the previous pages is *most* true about you?

This blocking is coming both from within and without. From the previous list of emotions that most men do not express, which emotions do you feel but have great difficulty expressing?

Second, imagine another way of dealing with feelings. Things don't have to be the way they are, either for us as individuals or for our society.

An examination of the Bible will reveal to us how culture-bound we are in regard to our emotional needs. We have already noted the magnificent emotional freedom Jesus expressed (in chapter 3). In this regard he was not unique, for many other Bible writers quite transparently exhibit the entire range of emotions we have discussed as often denied by men in our society.

Consider the clear expressing of emotions in the prayers of the psalmists. As you read this brief collection, note the tremendous range of feelings expressed here:

> Out of the depths, I cry to thee, O Lord!
> —Psalm 130:1

Why are you cast down, O my soul,

and why are you disquieted within me?
　　　　　　　　　　—Psalm 42:5
My tears have been my food day and night,
　while men say to me continually,
"Where is your God?"
　　　　　　　　　　—Psalm 42:3
　　Do I not hate them that hate thee, O LORD?
　　And do I not loathe them that rise up against thee?
　　I hate them with perfect hatred;
　　　count them my enemies.
　　　　　　　　　　—Psalm 139:21-22
(Apparently the psalmist found this outburst of anger helpful, for he
went on to pray beautifully in verses 23-24.)
　　　　　　　When my spirit is faint,
　　　　　　　　thou knowest my way.
　　　　　　　　—Psalm 142:3

　　　　　　　My soul longs, yea, faints
　　　　　　　　for the courts of the LORD;
　　　　　　　my heart and flesh sing for joy
　　　　　　　to the living God.
　　　　　　　　　　—Psalm 84:2
My God, my God, why hast thou forsaken me?
　Why art thou so far from helping me, from the words of
　my groaning?
　　　　　　　　　　—Psalm 22:1

　　　　　　Then our mouth was filled with laughter,
　　　　　　　and our tongue with shouts of joy;
　　　　　　　　—Psalm 126:2
　　How do you feel after reading and reflecting upon these brief passages
from the Psalms? Do you wish you could be in touch with your feelings
like that? express your emotions like that? find relief and joy in prayer
like that?
　　Emotions are the colors on the tapestry of living. Without emotions,
living is a white-grey-black type of existence. With emotions, life may
be experienced in living color. Imagine how rich your life can be with
many-splendored emotions coloring it!
　　Third, make the process visible. Find some ways to identify for
yourself what emotions you would like to express more fully and where
you can do this acceptably. Determine also where such expression
would not be acceptable. Perhaps you will want to write out your
impressions and examine them. Perhaps you will discover that you can

link some emotions and some activities. (For example, I might link anger with chopping wood, confusion with a long, quiet walk, etc.)

Fourth, find a trusted individual or small support group where you can comfortably test your assumptions, confide what you are discovering, experiencing, and bursting to share with someone else. Perhaps this will be a long time friend, of either sex, or your spouse. It is quite possible that you may not find anyone to whom you feel you can confide this information, or it may seem too frightening to do so. Then, you may want to find a competent mental health counselor and explore this subject with that counselor. However, the psalmists remind us that our prayer life offers us a richer opportunity to express emotions then most of us have yet discovered.

Fifth, experiment. Discover which of your blocked feelings you can most comfortably communicate and express with others. (Quite possibly it may be some of the positive ones, like empathy, self-disclosure, playfulness). Don't be alarmed if the expression of emotions feels awkward at first. Don't be overly upset if you are misunderstood. That's part of the risk.

But recognizing, experiencing, expressing, and sharing what is vibrant within you can be an enriching and fulfilling first step in changing your own male role expectations.

5

Charting the Wilderness

His Changing Sexuality

"We're a nation of sexual stammerers, and the more we keep quiet the more we will have to fear."—Dr. Mary Calderone

Asked why she prepared a massive study on male sexuality, Shere Hite responded, "The book was trying to ask how men feel about sexuality. The answer was they like it and treasure it—but at the same time they dislike it and feel very put upon by it." [1]

The above quotes well express the extremely confused state of men's sexuality. The confusion comes from at least three sources: (1) an overzealous misreading of what the Bible says about our sexuality; (2) a premature sexual revolution; and (3) the invasion of many problems from the stereotyped male role we have discussed in previous chapters. I'm not sure that I'm the one to unravel this troubled web, but I love to talk about sex anyway, so here goes.

What Does the Bible Really Say About Sex?

The Bible says that *(a)* sex is a beautiful, mysterious, sensual gift from God; and *(b)* this gift is subject to some rigorous controls. Both halves of that statement must be included to hear the Bible's whole witness on this subject. If we overemphasize one side of that statement and underemphasize the other half, we zealously misread the Bible. Let's consider each half of this statement in turn.

The Bible tells us that sex is God's beautiful creation. Genesis tells us that God looked on *all* that God had made "and behold it was very good" (Genesis 1:31). In Genesis 2, when God created woman and

47

man for each other, the man in delight exclaimed:

"This at last is bone of my bones and flesh of my flesh. . . ."
Therefore a man leaves his father and his mother and cleaves to his
wife and they become one flesh [a sexual and more-than-sexual image
to be sure]. And the man and his wife were both naked, and were
not ashamed (Genesis 2:23-25).

Innocence, delight, joy, beauty—sex as God intended it.

The Bible goes on to say that all our relationships are tainted by sin.
Though our sexual relationships are thus affected and are therefore not
all they could be, still the Bible portrays wonderful possibilities in love-
filled sexual relationships even after the Fall.

The writer of Proverbs counsels:

> . . . Rejoice in the wife of your youth,
>   a lovely hind, a graceful doe.
> Let her affection fill you at all times with delight,
>   be infatuated always with her love.
>   —Proverbs 5:18b-19

The Song of Solomon is a frank celebration of sexual love between
a man and a woman. It begins:

> Oh that you would kiss me with
>   the kisses of your mouth
> For your love is better than wine,
>   your anointing oils are fragrant . . .
>   —Song of Solomon 1:2

The description gets even better (better, that is, if you like flowery and
poetic, but explicit, celebration of sexual love).

These Bible passages, and others that could be added, describe the
sexual bond as a natural, powerful, beautiful experience between two
people who care for each other.

Further, when the Bible speaks of sexual intercourse, it frequently
uses a lovely term, the word "know." "Now Adam knew Eve his
wife, and she conceived . . ." (Genesis 4:1). Knowing refers here to
a deep interpersonal sharing, understanding, and fusing of bodies; what
a lovely way to speak of sexual intercourse! By contrast, run through
your mind the terms we use today for sexual intercourse. Don't they
have an angry, bitter, rasping sound in comparison? "_____ you"
(using any of the modern terms for intercourse in the blank) is almost
always a statement of anger and contempt. We don't catch that angry
mood when the Bible speaks of intercourse. Rather, it describes intercourse as a deep interpersonal sharing of two persons with each other.
Our Bible tells us that God made all aspects of us, including our

sexuality. It tells us further that God made our sexuality pure, innocent, and an expression of unity between man and woman. That is half of what the Bible says about sex.

The other half is a number of quite explicit commandments and teachings in regard to sex. To begin, the sixth commandment is, "Thou shalt not commit adultery" (Exodus 20:14). Married persons, should not have sexual intercourse outside marriage or with married persons other than their spouses. One passage (Leviticus 20:10-16) even prescribes the death penalty for this and goes on to forbid other sexual activity such as incest. The Bible speaks against fornication (sex before marriage) also, although it says much less about this. At the time this part of the Bible was written, persons married much younger and did not engage in dating and courtship as practiced in our culture; so premarital sex was not much of an issue.

Jesus goes on to hold before us a new righteousness that goes far beyond those laws. He speaks about the roving, consenting eye (Matthew 5:27-28). (I need a lot of forgiving grace on that one!) He speaks out against lax divorce standards, urging people not to divorce at all, or perhaps only if the partner has been unfaithful (Matthew 5:31-32). And he speaks against remarriage of divorced people (Matthew 5:31-32). One can conclude that the Bible teaches that this great gift of sex is to be channeled rigorously!

However, one other factor in the Bible's teaching about sex must be mentioned. The Bible often describes persons who practiced other sexual life-styles. For example, polygamy is rather frequently mentioned in the Old Testament. Prostitutes and adulterers are mentioned in Jesus' "family tree" (Matthew 1:3, 5, 6). Adulterers are forgiven in both the Old Testament and the New (John 8:1-12). Indeed, one adulterer was later mentioned as "a man after [God's] own heart" (1 Samuel 13:14). Permissive sexual behavior is spoken of as sin but not as THE sin and certainly not as the UNFORGIVABLE sin. Unfortunately some of our church forebears and leaders have overemphasized sexual offenses as THE sin. Grace and forgiveness are available to a person here as in every area of life.

That, in brief, is what the Bible teaches about sex. There are many legitimate questions as to how that relates to people in contemporary society, but for now we move on.

A Revolution or a Wilderness

Actually, the teachings contained in the previous pages are given much less consideration now than they were a generation or two ago. Some say that those who followed such sexual standards were motivated by a strong religious authority that is now eroding, and by fear that no longer applies. Actually the fear was threefold: "conception, infection, detection." These three problems have now been solved, the argument goes, so old sexual guidelines can go. Now it's "Do your own thing," or "If it feels good, do it," or "What is moral is what you feel good after." Some may choose a slightly more thoughtful, long-range method of deciding. However, the present emphasis seems to be on individuals deciding with little restriction or guidance from outside sources on what they, as two consenting adults, may do.

Some years ago, Vance Packard suggested that we are not in a sexual revolution, but rather we are in a sexual wilderness.[2] Rather than rebellion against all norms, confusion about which principles one should live by is what Packard discovered. He suggested that one could choose from several patterns of sexual behavior:

1. *Traditional repressive asceticism,* the basis of most official codes and laws. This viewpoint forbids any kind of sexual activity outside of marriage. It firmly links sex to procreation.

2. *Enlightened asceticism,* the belief that sex is good and positive. However, persons should first learn valuable lessons of self-control and discipline. Sex is one of the most basic areas in which this kind of self-mastery can be demonstrated.

3. *Humanistic liberalism,* the idea that "inflexible absolutes" should be rejected. Persons should consider the quality of the relationship and the consequences of the act when making sexual decisions.

4. *Humanistic radicalism,* the belief that present sexual codes of behavior are the result of "cultural engineering." Proponents of this view say that "with proper 'cultural engineering' the future young people can enjoy relatively complete sex freedom." Some persons with this view acknowledge that most people want love and warmth to accompany their sexual activities.

5. *Fun morality,* the viewpoint that sex is primarily fun. It is assumed that the more sex a person has, the sounder he or she will be psychologically. The chief proponent, Albert Ellis, feels premarital intercourse should be permitted freely. At times it should even be encouraged for well-informed, reasonably well-adjusted persons.

For the sake of completeness, I add the sixth option Packard noted, although I suspect the options in vogue are listed above.

6. *Sexual anarchy,* the position represented by the late René Guyon, who attacked chastity, virginity, and monogamy. Instead, he called for outlawing of all antisexual taboos. He wanted to wipe out all ideas that connect sexual activity with notions of immorality or guilt.[3]

Today, rather than rebelling against the sexual standards of church or society, persons need to ask what, if any, standards are in place, and how they can find the way that is right for them. As one man in *The Hite Report on Male Sexuality* comments, "What a hell of a way to live. Our sexual definitions and ideals are a mess, and they bring pain and sorrow to us all."[4]

The Male Role and Sex

As if all the confusion regarding principles of sexual behavior were not enough with which to contend, the expected male role also plays an important part in a man's sexual awareness and behavior. Do you remember those aspects of the male role we noted earlier: "No Sissy Stuff," "The Big Wheel," "The Sturdy Oak," and "Give 'em Hell"? Let's look at how these role expectations influence a man's sexuality.

"No Sissy Stuff"

The "No Sissy Stuff"role expectation triggers a great fear in many men, the fear called "homophobia," "the irrational fear or intolerance of homosexuality."[5] From boyhood on, the taunt, "What are you, a fag?" stirs the fear, *am I homosexual?* (I am not going to deal here with the existence of homosexuality, only with the fear of homosexuality in men who are predominantly heterosexual.)

Gregory Lehne notes that this fear called homophobia is based on many misconceptions about homosexual men: that homosexual men do not like women, that homosexual men are similar to women in appearance and psychological makeup and that they are thus effeminate, that homosexuals prefer and appropriately belong in certain professions (the ones most frequently mentioned are artist, beautician, florist, musician), that homosexuals often molest children. Each of these assumptions is clearly untrue for anyone who will take the time to study the factual information available. But if he does not correct his misconceptions, the fear-driven homophobic man cuts himself off from others and from himself. He is afraid of his sexuality and the unspeakable things this unbridled power might make him do.

Lehne notes that heterosexual males bear a lot of personal pain as a result of this irrational fear.

It impedes the formation of personal relationships. Men do not relate; they compete, at work and in their personal lives as well. It limits the types of relationships men have with other men. Though male bonds can be powerful and deeply satisfying, homophobic men are unwilling to admit love in their male friendships.

It can affect their heterosexual life. Homophobic men are more likely to have guilt and frustration over their sexuality. The two most frequent male sex problems, premature ejaculation and impotence, both of which nearly all men experience at times, can trigger even more fear within themselves and unwillingness to talk about sexual weakness, failure, or problems.

It can limit areas of interest or activity. A man may have a real interest in a subject that he will avoid because he is afraid it will imply homosexuality in himself.

It limits the free and open expression of affection and emotion by men toward other men.

Have you noticed one of the peculiarities of our culture in regard to this question: When is it permissible for two people to hug each other?
—children may hug each other.
—women may hug each other.
—a man and a woman may hug each other.
—the only men allowed to hug each other are athletes.
I guess they are permitted this because their athletic prowess makes their masculinity beyond question. For the rest of us men, there seems to be an implication that only homosexuals enjoy the hug of another man. Further, because of the same fears, some men limit expression of their emotions, a phenomenon which, as we said in the previous chapter, carries even heavier emotional hurt and loss.

It causes men to avoid non-sexual contacts (such as social or work contacts) with men known to be homosexual. Somehow the fear that someone might think they are homosexual is too great a threat to risk such contacts.[6]

You may strongly disagree with what I have said in the last few pages. If so, you have much company. I confess to a mystery here. Many of the authors and counselors I consulted felt that homophobia is indeed a basic and troubling factor that keeps men locked in repressive roles. However, most men with whom I visit totally deny this. When I presented this chapter to a men's group I was leading, they felt that I completely missed the boat in this section on homophobia. Two-thirds of the group said confidently that the fear of homophobia did not apply to them The remainder said that if they had this fear they did not recognize it.

I pondered this contradiction and finally decided to leave this section in. The men in the group may be right; fear of homosexuality may be no problem to them. Or it may be a fear buried so deep and with such threatening overtones that they are not ready to consider it. Does homophobia apply to you? You have to decide for yourself, but don't dismiss it too quickly. If homophobia is an unrecognized factor locked in men's subconscious, change will be all the more difficult.

"The Sturdy Oak," "The Big Wheel," "Give 'em Hell"

The male who attempts to be "The Sturdy Oak," with his air of toughness, confidence, and self-reliance, finds this attitude affecting his sex life. He does not communicate needs or desires to his partner, nor does he ask about hers. He assumes that somehow he ought to know her needs (and assumes that he does). Certainly, he finds it difficult to admit to anyone outside that partnership that he has any problems or needs any help. He buys into the sexual myth that as a male he ought to know!

The man who is caught up in "The Big Wheel" expectation, the need to succeed, be successful, be admired, may well find this influencing his sexuality as well. He may find himself preoccupied with numbers even in sex. There are many numbers that seem to concern men in sex—the size of the genitals, the number of "conquests" (a strange term for an intimate experience!), the number of contacts with a partner, the rate of recovery so that he is ready again. Although there are some experiences in life in which one should look for quality rather than quantity, that may not occur to the driven male.

In addition, "The Big Wheel" may be so goal oriented (whether it's orgasm, or mutual orgasm, or satisfying her, or satisfying himself) that he doesn't take time to delight in the process of getting there. Fear of failure (the flip side of which is the urgent need to succeed) can invade his bedroom, turning a playful, delightful experience into a time of somber testing. He also may come to view women as potential sexual partners or else not worthy of his interest at all. Women friends tell me that a fairly frequent experience for them is simply to be friendly and conversational with men they meet. Some men, however, read this behavior as a sexual come-on.

The "Give 'em Hell" aspect of the male role, the need to be aggressive, daring, perhaps even violent, contaminates sex for both men and women. A man may become the sexual aggressor when he doesn't want to be because he feels it is expected. Refusals become more serious than they need be. When force or fear becomes the motivation for sexual activity, it leaves anger and bitterness in its wake, not tenderness and closeness.

When one reflects on how male/female roles can get in the way of meaningful relating, one can experience wonder and joy that the sexual relationship between two people is even occasionally as beautiful as it was intended to be.

Beyond the Tangle

We men live in a whirlwind—a tornado?—caused by an overzealous misreading of what the Bible says about our sexuality, a premature sexual revolution, and the invasion of many problems from the stereotyped male role. How do we establish a healthy attitude toward sex? I think I begin to see the first few steps.

First, *I affirm and accept sex as a gift*. Of course, sex is much more than intercourse. It involves the way I feel about myself; it is also an intangible ingredient in my relating to both men and women. Like the emotions we discussed earlier, it adds zest, excitement, enjoyment to life. A man does not have to intend to bed a woman to enjoy the sparkle of even a brief meeting; our sexual nature and interest permeates all of our contacts with people.

I am aware that this is a male way of looking at things. I am told that often we males see sex when females do not. That's OK; we are each entitled to our own perceptions.

Second, I recognize that *I am my sexual response*. Men sometimes tend to view their sexual apparatus as something apart from themselves. They sometimes consider their feelings and their attitudes to be like a machine that can be "fixed" if it doesn't work right. I think we do much better when we buy into Herb Goldberg's perceptive conclusion:

> Every sexual response, no matter how seemingly insignificant, or under what circumstance, is a true statement of feeling and reaction towards one's partner, as well as being a revealing reflection of oneself as a person. Indeed, it is perhaps the most uncontrollable, powerful, clear and uncontaminated reflection of the overall feeling tone and quality of that relationship and of one's true self. It therefore always threatens to expose truths that one or both people would rather avoid.[7]

When Shere Hite asked men, "Why do you like intercourse?", the most frequent answers included physical closeness, sensations of masculinity, acceptance, and love. Only 3 percent mentioned orgasm. One man said, "It is the closest you can be to a person, and for a moment or an hour it overcomes the loneliness and separation of life." Hite concluded that perhaps intercourse is the only activity in which men feel free to express emotion.[8] Goldberg is telling us that it is also one place in which one cannot avoid one's own emotions.

My sexual response is an integral part of me and tells me much about me and about my relationships. It makes me more honest about me. My sexual feelings make it hard to avoid who I am. There is little place for phony piety or pretense. There is healthy realism here. I am my sexual response.

However, third, *I am more than my sexual response.* That response tells me some truth about me, but not the whole truth about me. For example, consider the common term used when a man is incapable of having intercourse. We say he is "impotent." The word "impotent" can be translated "without power." Now that's a ridiculous term to use in that circumstance, isn't it? A man may be sexually non-functioning, but he is certainly not without power, meaning, or significance as a person.

Or to give another example, the surgeon tells the man who has had a vasectomy, "Consider yourself permanently sterile." Permanently sterile? One definition of "sterile" is "unproductive of results, fruitless." I fear that sometimes a man so directly connects his "ability to produce results" to his sexuality, that he avoids this sensible, painless, procedure when he could enjoy being worry-free from siring an unexpected child.

Quite beyond these considerations, I am more than my sexuality. I have meaning, importance, satisfactions, goals—quite apart from my sexuality. The important task for me is to find the proper place sex has within my whole being, my whole life structure. There are times when it is urgently important, and times when it is simply part of my personal atmosphere. I need to find sex's proper place in my life without making it the ONLY consideration—as a number of movies and other media seem to imply—and without denying or suppressing/repressing it.

In this connection a recent survey was conducted by two sociologists, Dr. William Smith of the University of Houston and Dr. Patricia Miller of Smith College. They interviewed nearly two thousand males between the ages of eighteen and forty-nine and asked, "What is most important to you for a happy life?" Their answers in order of importance were (1) health; (2) love; (3) peace of mind; (4) family life; (5) work; (6) friends; (7) respect from others; (8) education. And then after these, in ninth place, they put sex!![9]

The results of this survey make me suspect that men have gone after sex when what they were really looking for was something else—companionship, reassurance, self-esteem, intimacy. I'm not saying that sex cannot be part of any of those, but sex as a substitute for any of those is a mistake and a disappointment.

There is a potentially liberating discovery in these two very simple insights: I am my sexual response; I am much more than my sexual response.

Fourth, *I choose the values* by which I express my sexuality. No longer do I simply accept an outside authority uttering absolutes about a mysterious, unexamined part of my life. Rather, I affirm my faith teachings about the divine origin of sex. I become aware of all the sex ethics options being explored in my pluralistic society. I become intentional about my life and its purpose as God has entrusted it to me. I become equally intentional about the relationships in my life. Then I choose my sexual values and live them out.

I will probably need to be quite "up front" about my sexual values and life-style since there are so many styles around. And I pursue my Christian values with the awareness that our God forgives and restores failures here as in every other area of life.

Vance Packard was right. It is a sexual wilderness. However, in the overcast sky above, a few stars gleam to help me choose my direction.

6

Breaking Through the Relationship Barrier

His Friendships—"Buddyships"

I must admit I have a more difficult time getting acquainted with men than with women. A number of times when I have met a man for the first time, almost exactly the same exchange takes place:

He: "What do you do for a living?"

I: "I'm a pastor."

Then he gives either or both of the next two responses.

He: "How large is your congregation, Reverend?" or
   "Well, I'm Lutheran."

And then, awkward silence. We have spoken of occupation, numbers, and self-label, and we have no more to say to one another. I've wondered if my profession puts a distance between me and many men, but I'm told that first meetings of other men go very similarly. Unless I can get beyond those categories and ask him about a subject that interests him, or try talking about something that I hope he likes, our conversation is over.

I don't remember ever having that get-acquainted exchange when I met a woman for the first time. Maybe I tried harder, but I think there is more than that. Somehow we seem to fall more easily into finding mutual interests to explore together. It shouldn't be hard to find some points of contact with any person. I love to talk about places I've lived, travels, my family, hobbies, jokes, the things I'm good at, etc. In all these there are certainly some points of contact between two people. I seem to find that bridge between persons easier with women than with men.

And so I was not surprised to discover that many men have difficulty

57

in forming friendships with men. Herb Goldberg relates that while interviewing many men about interpersonal relationships, he asked them if they had any close male friends. The usual response was, "No, why should I?" He says they seemed to see their isolation and lack of friendships with other men as quite normal, not even something to examine or question.[1]

Daniel Levinson and associates made a similar discovery in their depth study of forty men.

> . . . we would say that close friendship with a man or woman is rarely experienced by American men . . . . Most men do not have an intimate male friend of the kind that they recall fondly from boyhood or youth. Many men have had casual dating relationships with women, and perhaps a few complex love-sex relationships, but most men have not had an intimate non-sexual friendship with a woman. We need to understand why friendship is so rare, and what consequences this deprivation has for adult life.[2]

In her book, *About Men,* Phyllis Chesler includes an essay misnamed "Brotherhood," for actually she writes about the absence of brotherhood. She reports that when she questions men about "male friendships and other male 'bondings,' men often stare at me, fall silent, accuse me of naiveté—and laugh."[3] They seem to recall betrayals by men more vividly than friendships. They speak of those who have made it to the top as "top dog," or "chief ape," or "big gun," and she wonders why men unconsciously ascribe qualities of animals and weapons to successful human beings. She contends that "when one listens to the answers men give to questions about 'male bonding,' it becomes obvious that most men expect only competition and betrayal from other men."[4] Though they obviously need sympathy and support from each other, says she, they rarely expect it or find it. The men with whom she visited even rejected the notion that army buddies were as close or as lasting as one would expect from watching Hollywood war movies.

A forty-year-old politician told her that he had political buddies, persons with whom he exchanged favors.

> But they're not my friends. . . . Power isn't kept by a system of friendships. It's kept by how fast you can move with a change of time or need . . . how easily you can drop another guy when he's wrong or going under. . . . The people I *relax* with are in other areas. . . . I have allies and I have enemies, and I have my family. I have no *friends.*[5]

She reports the conversation of a man in his mid-thirties describing what happens when two men meet for the first time:

> A lot of things go on. It's like two dogs circling each other and checking each other out . . . . his economic scale. Is he manly? Is he tough? . . .

Can he help me? Can I help him? Is he gonna use me? Am I using him? Does he know a lot of pretty women? All these things take place in the course of a handshake. . . . Friendship could take place after some of these questions are resolved. After the competition is eliminated or channeled or accepted.

It seems to me that generally when you first meet, men are vying to see who's going to have the top position. . . .[6]

A male in his late twenties has a more direct way of relating:

You can become friends after a street fight, if nobody gets hurt too badly. It's acting out the competitiveness that a fight can mellow out. . . . That's one of the ways that friendship can develop. You see, once you clear that air there, once you find out if the other man can fight, you can team up if it's a beneficial thing to do.[7]

From these and other interviews she draws the sweeping conclusion:

Men "bond" together only because (other) men are the deadliest killers of men on earth. Men "bond" only temporarily, to avoid, or to commit, savage acts of betrayal or humiliation of other men. Male-bonding is about the lengths to which men are willing to go to gain male approval, or rather, to avoid male violence; male-bonding is about the male craving to inherit power from real or surrogate father-figures—power at least over women, if not over other men."[8]

Is she right? Is that the terror and violence that motivates all of our relationships with other men?

Herb Goldberg notes that one of the ironies of our culture is that men seemingly can come comfortably close together only when they share a common enemy or target.[9] So the closest bonding among men seems to be in:

—street gangs, who group to fight other gangs.
—athletic teams, who organize to defeat other teams.
—armed forces, in which the "target" or "enemy" may change from time to time, and may include the commanding officer, the "system," or the nation one's own country is opposing.
—business, in which the organization needs to beat the opposition.

This bonding is very temporary indeed; when the competition goes away, the reason for the group also vanishes. Since these competitive opportunities will decrease as one grows older, the older man is apt to suffer from the lack of even the appearance of male friendships, unless some other basis for friendship is found.

In an intensive survey on the subject of friendship itself, Joel Block made similar discoveries—that men seem to expect rivalry and betrayal, not sympathy or devotion from other males. His survey showed that eighty-four percent of the men interviewed did not feel free to disclose themselves fully to other men. Ninety-two percent had not had a frank sexual discussion with a buddy. Since succeeding and getting ahead seemed to be such an important consideration for the men he interviewed, they were not about to reveal any doubt, uncertainty, or weakness. They would rather be seen by other men as "confident, successful, and sexually assured" than risk being known otherwise by a man who might be a friend—but might also be an adversary.[10]

At this point you may be reflecting on your own experience and saying, "I'm different. Unlike those men just described, I have lots of friends." And probably you do. But the question is, have any of those friendships developed to the point that they sustain you as a person?

Joel Block discovered several types of friendship:

Convenience friends, people for whom you will do a favor and who will do a favor for you. Neighbors or co-workers who will water your plants for you while you are away or do other such favors are convenience friends.

Doing-Things Friends, persons with whom you share interest in a particular activity, a sport, hobby, membership in a service organization, etc. Such friends are unlikely to develop deep intimacy.

Milestone Friends, friends that we treasure from a particular time in life—high school, military service, college, etc. At one time we shared our ups and downs with these persons, and we love to see them occasionally to recall those times.

Mentor Friends, persons who influenced us through teaching, modeling, guiding, helping us get started, helping us make sense out of things. Often these friendships cool when they move from a teacher-student relationship to a more equal basis.

Part-of-a-Couple Friends, the spouse of your friend or your wife's friend, in which the spouse's friendship is primary and you "go along for the ride."

Good Friends, the persons to whom we are especially close, that we see often (if possible), and count on when we are in need. These are persons with whom we share our private lives, with whom we celebrate our joys and triumphs, that sustain us when we are lonely, sad, or depressed.[11]

Block quotes a young woman who expressed what this latter type of friendship meant to her:

> There are friends I have grown up with and with whom I have shared important parts of my life—my memories, our hometown, our youth. And then there are friends you meet later in life with whom you share more than a common history; with these friends there is a real exchange of thoughts and feelings. These are the people who will endure your ecstasies,

who will fly with you. With these friends you are able to break down barriers, to go beyond common experience.

When I am with such an exceptional companion, time stands still. It is for these people I reserve the glowing hours, too good not to share. I don't need cigarettes, food, or liquor; I get caught up in the experience. We seem to be parts of the same mind. The next day and for several days I feel more energetic, very optimistic. The effort of sharing, of getting involved, leaves me with an increase in power.[12]

She might have added that such friends can help you "make it through the night" when sadness, grief, disappointment, or depression would otherwise overwhelm you.

Goldberg notes that men seem unable to share the good or the bad. They don't seem to be comfortable sharing their failures, disappointments, or anxieties. They don't want to be seen as losers or crybabies. They also seem to be unready to share their happiness or success for fear of appearing boastful.[13]

Block discovered that three-fourths of the men he interviewed had doing-things friends, convenience friends, or mentor friends. Many fewer had good friends even coming close to the depth we just described.[14]

Why Do Men Have So Few Deep Friendships?

Reasons why men do not have deep friendships are not hard to find. For one thing, lack of time, heavy work schedule, and increased mobility cut people off from one another. A friendship needs to be given time and loving attention. But the press of time, primarily from work, is a common experience for men. Also, frequent moves from one part of the country to another uproot us and our potential friendships.

Further, marriage and family commitments can get in the way of other friendships. Some of us have had the unspoken assumption in marriage: "You (my spouse) don't need any other friends. I'll be your best friend. I'm all you need." Such an assumption puts an unfair strain on the marriage (by expecting too much of it) and may cut a person off from old friends or potentially enriching new friendships.

Then children come into the marriage. A man expects that he will be a friend to his children. He will show interest in them and will attend the events in which they participate or perform. All of this puts his life in more of a time bind and may lead him to allow friendships outside the family to erode.

The previous reasons why men have few if any friendships are true. However, they are by no means the complete explanation. We must look deeper.

Still another reason is that many men lack the skills of developing friendships. Either by temperament or training or both, we men may be quite shy, timid, private. We may feel we lack conversational skills. We may hesitate to reach out in risky interpersonal situations. We may long for friendships but be afraid to attempt one. We may have attempted to form friendships, failed, and given up. I personally recall the painful experience of admiring a man and trying very hard to become friends with him, only to discover he didn't want to be friends with me. The memory still smarts. Lack of courage and interpersonal skills may hold us back.

Lack of a sense of self-worth (what would I have to bring to a relationship?) can hold a man back from looking for friendship. His awareness that he needs space and privacy may cause him to overemphasize this need for privacy and under-invest in developing friendships. The ever-present male need to be in control may hamper a man's willingness to risk vulnerability and mutual trust in friendship.

On the other hand, the urgency of needing friends may hamper the search. It may cause a man to come on too strongly and frighten potential friends away.

Further still, we may hold back from friendships with men because of homophobia, that fear we mentioned in the previous chapter, fear that we either may be homosexual, or even be considered homosexual. Robert Brannon recalls:

> In college the affection and caring I felt for my three roommates worried me because I could sense it wasn't really *all that* different from the affection I felt for the girlfriends I knew best and liked most. If the truth be known, I cared more genuinely for my male friends at this time than for any female I knew. What's worse, when we were sprawled out somewhere watching T.V. or reading, and our legs or arms would touch comfortably, it was . . . well, pleasant! . . .''[15]

He feared this closeness and drew back from it because of his secret fear that he was a "latent homosexual."

But the biggest of all barriers to men's friendship with each other is COMPETITION. Phyllis Chesler discovered that men expected only competition from each other and were rarely disappointed. We compete in games (and winning even insignificant contests seems to become more important than the fun of playing them), compete for women, compete for grades in school, compete for jobs, compete for advancement, compete for "success." And so we don't form friendships with men more financially successful than we; it will look as if we're using them. And we don't form friendships with those on the same level; we may compete for the next promotion and don't want to make them feel bad when we get it. And we don't talk about ourselves to companions;

they may discover our weaknesses, beat us out, and then we will feel bad when they are promoted instead.

This looks silly and petty on paper, but every student of men's relationships will tell you that the barrier of competition is real. It boils down to this: you can't be a competitor and a real friend to a person at the same time. You have to choose which you want most.

Breaking the Friendship Barrier

I guess I'm one of the fortunate men. I have a number of meaningful friendships with both men and women. I'm going to tell you about two of those friendships, both with men, to show how one can break the friendship barrier. Let me say that at the time these friendships started, I was as shy, timid, and ill-equipped for friendship as any average male.

I met Lee when I was seventeen. We were assigned to be roommates at a church youth convention. Our first impression of each other was identical: "He's okay, but nobody you could have fun with." We could not have been more wrong. A year later we met again at college, where we were classmates for four years. Lee often tells people, "We were the perfect college partnership; I had the car and Dick had the brains." True, but our relationship was more complex than that. We often double-dated and consoled each other over the reverses in our romances. (He was and still is more skillful in relationships with women than I.) We participated together in choirs and plays. We were part of a gang that could reduce the most important, solemn subject to ridiculous proportions and see the humor in it. And so we laughed and laughed together. We played one year of football together; he was the one that introduced me to that ill-fated football team of which I spoke earlier, but I have forgiven him for that. We shared freely what little money or food that we had.

Graduation day brought an empty feeling when I saw him and his wife, Barb, pull their trailer out of town headed for grad school at Berkeley. I would shortly leave for Boston. It would have been one of those "milestone friendships" after that, and nothing more. But he did not let the friendship die. He found ways to keep in touch. Fortunately, after theological school we wound up just a couple of hundred miles apart for a while. He'd call on the phone to ask my opinion, just to chat, or to see how I was. We'd invite each other to be guest leaders in each other's churches, which gave us more opportunity to be together. With his directness, he'd probe into areas of my life I'd just as soon ignore, but I trusted him; so I'd let him probe. I learned and grew. He kept me laughing. Once when he was coming to visit, one of my daughters asked if she could go with me to meet him at the airport. When I asked her why, she responded, "Because you guys are nuts." She was right; Lee draws out that playful, humorous side of me, a side I don't experience or show as much as I'd like. Lee and Barb have always been most generous with me, entertaining me in their home or out on the town many times. What a great feeling it was when enough prosperity came my way that I could treat them once in a while! We're a thousand or so miles apart again, and the phone is our most basic link nowadays. Sometimes I pick it up. Sometimes he does. But we both know we are there for the other.

I met Ron when I was twenty-three. Lee introduced us; he and Ron were classmates at Berkeley. I helped Ron get a job near me once simply because he was the friend of a friend. From that geographical closeness, we enjoyed some couple and family times together. And we would sometimes have lunch together to talk about work problems. I remember vividly a particular night after we had known each other a few years. Ron was a guest in our home; everyone but he and I had gone to bed. He started to talk and share seriously about some hurting areas of his life—areas about which he had only joked with me before. He talked about these far into the night. I guess I listened caringly, trustworthily. I know I cared about his hurt and had confidence in him to deal with it. Out of that came a deeper trust relationship so that now we can talk over absolutely anything or ask anything of one another.

Before I moved several hundred miles away from Ron, we saw each other fairly frequently at regional gatherings of our denomination, and we almost always found a few hours for pizza, updating each other on our lives, and laughs.

We used to take an annual "study leave" together. (Some who knew us best had a hard time believing that was what we did.) We would get a room near a seminary library. During the day we would each read on topics we wished to pursue, pausing every couple of hours to tell the other what we had discovered about the theme or issue we were exploring. One time, we planned a sermon series together. The effectiveness of that effort showed both of us that two heads are better than one, if only we male individualists can learn to collaborate. But the best part of those study leaves were the evenings, when we would go to see a movie or play, or enjoy a leisurely dinner and good conversation. I cannot possibly describe the renewal and strength I gained from sharing such experiences with someone I enjoyed and cared about.

My relationship with Lee is different from that with Ron. I would describe my relationship with Lee as more intense (although he's mellowing now that he's getting older) and with Ron as more relaxed. But in each relationship we have found permission to be who we are and care about the other person as he is.

I have learned several things from this mental exploration of friendship:

1. There is real joy and power in friendships which are well worth the risk, effort, and investment one puts into them.

2. If you are willing to risk, you can move deeper into friendship than you may have thought.

3. Friendships need both time to grow and effort to cultivate them. Herb Goldberg has suggested that if one is going to develop the kind of friendship he calls "buddyship," one which is deep as well as spontaneous, the relationship with his potential "buddy" will probably pass through four stages:

a) The manipulative or instrumental phase. Two people need each other and "use" each other to the benefit of both. This is not necessarily bad. I relate in an instrumental way to my barber, my mechanic, my dentist. However, the relationship is incomplete. This is the place where most male relationships begin and end.

b) The companionship phase. Two persons share in some specific activities, like golfing, playing cards, etc. Usually conversation stays on the activity or other "safe" topics, but it does provide the contact and opportunity for a deeper relationship to develop. This may be a mutual testing period to see if a closer friendship can develop.

c) The friendship phase. Competitiveness is sublimated. There is pleasure in just being with the other. Friends offer each other "mutual aid, compassion, and a willing readiness to be there in an emergency. [They] will lend money or other valued objects." [16] This phase involves the whole person.

d) The "buddyship" phase. This phase is reached when two persons have successfully gone through an emergency together. Each has revealed his vulnerabilities to the other, and deep trust has thus developed. [17]

Herb Goldberg describes "buddyship" as the most profound male-to-male relationship. Buddies are free to be either teacher or student to each other. They rejoice in each other's development and expanded skills, for they have learned to get beyond competition. With a buddy, one can also admit to feeling weak, can act foolish, can be vulnerable. One trusts and knows such feelings will be accepted, shared, understood. Buddies share both emotional and material resources.

Buddies have learned to live beyond the usual "roles." They can be silly, stupid, childlike, affectionate in the presence of each other—sides of themselves they may not feel safe to show anyone else.

For the most part we lack "buddyship" skills in our culture. We somehow have not cultivated such skills in males. "Buddyship" requires time investment, the same sort of persistence one gives to developing one's career, the willingness to work through crises. It also requires the awareness that since one is blazing an important new trail of meaning, such male-to-male closeness will be frequently misunderstood.[18]

4. In friendship you need to learn both to give and to receive, to reach out and to respond to the other person's reaching. A most important thing you have to give is honest information about yourself, your feelings, your needs, your experience. But just as important is your acceptance of the other person as he reveals himself to you.

5. Even with all that effort comes the discovery that friendship is essentially a gift. It should always be viewed with awe and gratitude, for that sort of love is always a matter of grace.

Biblical Faith and Friendship

The Bible speaks with a clear voice on this subject of friendship. It offers us the modeling of a marvelous friendship of two males, Jonathan and David.

Jonathan should have had every reason to hate David. They were competitors. It began to appear that what should have been Jonathan's (the throne of his father, Saul) was going to be David's instead. But rather than respond with hatred, Jonathan remained strong in his earlier friendship. We read, "And Jonathan made David swear again by his love for him; for he loved him as he loved his own soul" (1 Samuel 20:17). Jonathan agreed to be David's spy in Jonathan's father's court, and he secretly told David to flee because Saul was angry. In one final secret meeting, "David rose from beside the stone heap and fell on his face to the ground, and bowed three times; and they kissed one another, and wept with one another until David recovered himself" (1 Samuel 20:41).

Shortly after that, both Saul and Jonathan were killed in battle. In his grief, David uttered a lament and spoke of Jonathan.

> Jonathan lies slain upon thy high places.
> I am distressed for you, my brother Jonathan;
> very pleasant have you been to me;
> your love to me was wonderful,
> passing the love of women.
> —2 Samuel 1:25b-26

David was a man's man, and yet he expressed friendship and love like that. Jonathan transcended all the usual competitions and intrigues to love his friend David to the death. Such a friendship beckons to us and calls us to deeper trust, love, and companionship than we had imagined possible.

And friendship with God is also available to the believer. The 139th Psalm begins:

> O LORD, thou hast searched me and known me!
> Thou knowest when I sit down and when I rise up;
>   thou discernest my thoughts from afar.
> Thou searchest out my path and my lying down,
>   and art acquainted with all my ways.
> —Psalm 139:1-2

The psalm explores God's presence in all of the world, in guilt, in anger, in one's conception, in guidance for life; it concludes with a prayer for God's friendship not only now but forever, "lead me in the way everlasting" (Psalm 139:24b).

The Bible also holds forth the ideal of the community of believers being "the body of Christ," members one of another, so that "if one member suffers, all suffer together" (1 Corinthians 12:26a). One-on-one friendships, an individual with his God, the Christian community supporting one another—all witness that God's gracious will for us is deeper friendship and community than any of us have yet found.

The male who is this new person will love expressively and freely. This new freedom will enrich both him and his world.

7

Finding Help from an Unexpected Source

The Message for Men in Women's Liberation

The women's movement has made women aware of the roles assigned them in society. This has triggered men's consciousness about their roles. Women have become aware of the inequity, unfairness, and discrimination in the roles assigned them. In turn men have discovered that aspects of their roles are not satisfying either. In these discoveries is ferment for a new society.

That new society will not come automatically; such change never comes easily. Change triggers fear, anger, and other difficult feelings. Resistance occurs all along the way to a more just, humane society.

A man attempting to build a new life-style needs to consider feminist hopes as well as the feminist critique of society. Those hopes and criticisms are closely bound up with his own.

The aim of the women's movement is deceptively simple, "sexual equality in all spheres of life."[1] Joyce McCarl Nielsen suggests that some of the more specific goals arising from this aim include the following: adequate (in number and quality) child-care centers run by both women and men; equal opportunity in employment; equal opportunity in education; legalized available abortion; passage of the Equal Rights Amendment; nonsexist language and images in all forms of media; prevention of rape; availability of medical self-help; maternity leaves in employment and education; nonsexist educational material; nonsexist child-rearing practices; and the end of spouse and child abuse.[2]

Letha Scanzoni and Nancy Hardesty passionately argue for a women's liberation from a Christian point of view. They think of liberation as "a state of mind." In this state of mind, a woman sees herself as Jesus

69

Christ sees her. She becomes aware that she is a person created in God's image. She senses God's will for her is that she should be free and whole. She can grow and learn to use fully all the gifts, abilities, and talents God has given her as a unique person.[3]

They continue their Christian apologetic by suggesting:

> Liberation means an end to the self-hatred women have been taught, an end to the hatred we project on other women. Often women resist liberation because we have been taught that our bodies are weaker, our powers of reasoning defective, our intellects lighter, our skills inferior, our emotions frivolous. And we have believed our teachers. We suffer from low self-esteem and no self-confidence. Women's liberation has been termed an "identity crisis." Women are beginning to ask, "Who am I? What does it mean to say that *I* am created in the image of God?" Christ commanded us to love others as ourselves, but we women have been taught to despise ourselves. And so we have mistrusted other women. . . .[4]

I am amazed to hear that women feel they have been taught self-hatred, but one of my feminist friends affirms this. Out of her deep involvement in the women's movement she tells me, "I am more alive, I like myself better, and I am more centered than I have ever been in my life." She is experiencing a greater connection between her inner self and her outer actions.

When I ponder the above statements of Nielsen, Scanzoni, Hardesty, my response as a man goes something like this: I'm all for equality. While I might debate a point or two of Ms. Nielsen's list of the women's movement objectives, I have daughters, a sister, a mother, a wife, and women friends for whom I want the best. Be patient; if I still have trouble believing some of what you say, remember that I'm on your side.

Then, when I begin to absorb the proposed radical changes in a society where I've grown rather comfortable, when I begin to hear some of the accusations and name calling, I find myself on the defensive and in a turmoil.

Let's look at the potential losses and the potential benefits *for us men* that are arising out of the women's movement.

Potential Losses for Men from the Women's Movement

A minor casualty is the loss of traditions regarding how to treat one another. What is courtesy, what is graciousness? How do you address a person? What terms are proper? What terms are condescending or sexist? Do I stand up when women come into the room? hold the door for a woman? pick up the tab when I eat with a woman friend? I used to know what to do in these situations; I don't any more. It's no great difficulty to learn a new set of amenities, but there is no universal agreement on the new ones as there was on the old. Other men speak of losing a sense of ease or comfortableness with women. One man tells me, "I used to enjoy my spontaneous humor, but once in a while, one of my comments offends someone. So now, I sort out everything before I say it, and I've lost my timing." I must confess to having lived enough years to mourn those kinds of losses.

A much greater loss that many of us men feel is the unjust blame that we feel is heaped on us. We were born into this society, too. Although we didn't create all the injustices that may exist today, we have to deal with some lively angers directed at us. With help from the women's movement a woman gets in touch with her long repressed rage. In the excitement of this movement a man may be described as "the oppressor, victimizer, abuser, user, exploiter, chauvinist, sexist pig." On the other hand, the woman is described as "the oppressed, victimized, abused, used, exploited, maligned, passive, blameless, helpless victim."[5]

As one man put it to me, "I'm tired of being held accountable for all the evils of society. Whatever I do, I'm wrong. I was the oppressor when minority groups wanted more rights. Now I'm the oppressor in regard to women. You can't be right. Take the issue of wife abuse and child abuse. If you express concern, you are guilty. If you don't, you're calloused. It's a losing battle."

Quite probably, in the process of working in liberation issues, some exaggerated and unfair accusations are thrown at men in general. Herb Goldberg recalls attending a panel discussion during which a feminist speaker gave an example of how men exploit women: forcing them to have babies to satisfy the men's egos. Mr. Goldberg reports a feeling of astonishment as he heard that. He had been raised to believe that women wanted to have children, that this was a special form of fulfillment. He had been trained to believe that it would be selfish and unmanly to resist a woman's desire for motherhood. His experience as a therapist also made him aware of the many women who wanted to be mothers and who brought their passive or resistant partners along into the parental enterprise. The accusation that men forced women to have children made no sense at all to him.[6] However, since males have tended to feel totally responsible for the success, welfare, and happiness of their families, such accusations tend to make them feel guilty. They feel guilty whether the accusation is correct or not.

It seems to me that when these accusations fly, a man needs to ask two questions. Is this accusation true in general? Is this accusation true about me? He should learn what he can and change what he can from the answers to those questions. He should by no means dismiss the whole movement because some assertions made by persons within it seem to him to be extreme.

My wife has reason for outrage. We are both mid-lifers, but she is just starting her career and I am at the peak of mine. She needs lots more training in her field, while I am well trained in mine. We both work hard and try to do good work, but she gets about half the pay I do. She has reason for anger, but I am not the oppressor, and I don't like to be called one. To the extent that we bought into the usual cultural pattern—to marry young, educate the husband, and have babies— we are both oppressed and we are both the oppressors.

And still another sense of loss for men is that some of this displaced anger impacts on their marriages. One man humorously put it this way, "I feel as though my wife and I are standing on a street corner. A truck goes by and sprays her with slush. It makes her so mad that she turns and hits *me* with her purse." Others fail to see the humor when marital tensions are heightened by these extra angers. Of course, no one reason causes the rapid increase in the divorce rate and the breakup of the traditional family. Still, the loss of family stability is to be mourned for all the pain it brings to those involved.

The loss of mutually understood ways for men and women to relate to each other,
    The burial of self-esteem under a huge pile of anger,
        accusation, and blame,
        The destruction of some fragile marriages and
            families.

These are some of the losses men feel from the impact of the women's movement.

Potential Gains for Men from the Women's Movement

But all is by no means loss. Herb Goldberg, while critical of some of the extravagant claims by certain persons in the women's movement, suggests that men should accept and embrace the women's movement for the life-expanding possibilities it can offer them.[7] He suggests further that men have nothing to lose from feminism but guilt and fantasies of what women supposedly are. He believes that the feminist movement represents a new attitude, the desire of women to act as whole persons rather than as stereotypes. The feminist message is: "We refuse to relate like children any more."[8] All well and good, says Goldberg, so long as the man does not become the empty echo of this new movement. The man may be willing to accept extra responsibilities or redistributed ones, but he needs to ask fair questions. "What do I gain from all this change? Or is there only loss for me?"

Warren Farrell and Herb Goldberg each note a number of the possible gains, which I will summarize.

First, the basis for marriage and all love relationships between a man and a woman can be enhanced and become more genuine. This may come from many sources.

They can get beyond the too frequent old pattern: "He married a sex object. She married a standard of living." [9]

If both have gained economic independence, they can make the decision to remain married or to separate in an atmosphere of responsible freedom. They will not stay together because they are trapped either by guilt or financial dependence.

Sexual interest may heighten in this freer, unstereotyped relationship. Abraham Maslow's study of human personalities contains the discovery that a man experiences much greater sexual fulfillment with a woman who is alive to herself and is developing her full personal potential. [10]

Both the male and female partner are freed from the expectation of being the sole source of his or her partner's happiness. Rather, marriage partners are seen as significant persons with whom to share the highs and lows. But each is not responsible for the other's ecstasies or gloom. Each takes responsibility for his or her own feelings.

Both the male and female partner can allow the other more autonomy in personal life. Since neither is the sole source of the other's satisfaction, both feel more free to let loose so that each can pursue what is fulfilling.

All of these rich possibilities can actually take place if each member of a couple accepts the other's growth and worth, if both are sensitive to the other's needs and to their commitment to each other, and if both partners keep talking with each other about what they are experiencing, wanting, needing, or missing in their relationship. With this kind of behavior they are moving into the scary new world of "marriage by intention" rather than "marriage by habit."

Second, there is the potential for enhanced home and family life. When we have equal pay for men and women and thus more economic autonomy, then perhaps both parents could work less and spend more quality time with their children—not just the "poison hours" from 6 to 8 P.M. when young children are tired, hungry, and ready for bed. Or the husband and wife could determine who would take the time away from work to be with children and care for them.

Also, all the other household responsibilities can be readjusted in a way that is free from traditional sex stereotypes. What tasks are "mine, yours, ours" can be renegotiated on the basis of what is most liked and least disliked by each. The traditional stereotypes of "man's work," and "woman's work" can go.

Third, the woman's movement can bring a liberating influence to a man's employment. If his spouse were earning equal wages, many freeing things could happen for him.

Escape from the role of "sole breadwinner" would release him from the subtle power his employer has over him. If a man is the sole source of money for his family, fear of losing his job can keep him from speaking out on moral issues at work, from facing up to unfair bosses, from taking risks. Shared responsibility for family economics could free him from the inhibiting fear of losing his job.

He could feel free to pursue a low-paying job that holds more interest for him rather than dutifully persisting in something that pays well but holds little interest for him.

He could feel free to take a year or two off from work to retrain for a new career or to pursue a non-compensating interest or to care for a household. Men who have been able to take such a break—even a brief one—tell me that they go back to work with renewed enthusiasm and enjoyment.

Fourth, a man may be set free to let go of some of the most confining aspects of sex-role stereotypes.

He can let go of the male compulsion to assume all responsibility, to direct the lives of all around him. Men's being in control of everything has not always worked anyway, and so it can well be let go. As a male, I don't have to be in control anymore. At the same time, I can influence the lives of those around me as they influence me. At first this may feel like a loss to some males, but in time it will feel much more like freedom.

As artificial standards of masculinity decrease, a man may lose his fear of homosexuality with all the inhibitions on free expression of emotion, love, friendship that this fear has carried with it.

Fifth, a man may gain much more from listening carefully as he relates to women on a new basis. No longer the one who needs to have an opinion, or *the* opinion on every subject, he may be intrigued by the discoveries of fresh new insights. He may find himself fascinated by individual women to whom he now relates as individuals not sex objects. And he may be equally interested in the feminist view of a new society.

Sixth, it is possible for a man to experience an easier and happier retirement. Rather than living a life with one focus, his work, which becomes abruptly terminated, he has the opportunity to live a full, varied life. As a result he has less difficult adjustments at retirement.

The shared responsibilities of marriage and the wider interests that this sharing has made possible give him ample opportunities to develop a rich retirement.

Does all of this seem unlikely, fanciful, remote? Perhaps it is. Does it seem impossible? It is by no means impossible. The Christian vision of humanity set free is very closely related to this kind of visioning. Paul's visionary statement, "There is neither male nor female for you are all one in Jesus Christ" (Galatians 3:28), contains the seed of this vision. He further says, "For freedom Christ has set us free; stand fast therefore, and do not submit again to a yoke of slavery. . . . For you were called to freedom . . . only do not use your freedom as an opportunity for the flesh, but through love be servants one for another" (Galatians 5:1, 13). These words were originally written to address another denial of freedom, and yet they stand as a call to full liberation and the full development of individuals. This Scripture is also a guide to remind Christian men and women to be more gentle and understanding with each other as they work through these issues.

Herb Goldberg suggests, "The growth of men depends on the growth of women, and vice versa, in order for the sexes to experience the full potential of themselves and each other." [11] Perhaps he overstates it. We males and females can quite probably grow without each other. It will be much more pleasant and joyful if we grow individually, but grow together.

Although there are some losses to be mourned in the changes we are experiencing, there is an incredibly beautiful gain in the freedom to be ourselves.

8

Not Robert, or Dagwood, but You

Changing Fatherhood

At the time I write this, my children are 21, 19, and 16. Two of them live more than a thousand miles away from me. The third will graduate from high school in two years and probably go her separate way as well. Increasingly, she has less time to spend with me as she plans her life within her own busy world. I am about to be fired as a father—fired, that is, as far as day-to-day direct involvement with and influencing of my children.

As a matter of fact, on the very day I write this, my youngest daughter is nervously making preparations for her first prom. I cannot believe my eyes—a child yesterday, a beautiful young woman in an evening gown today. I willingly turn from my typewriter to swap stories with her about dances in her day and mine and to go with her to buy a boutonniere. Something opens before her tonight—formal social events and adult ways of meeting and relating. Something closes on me tonight—the illusion that any of my "children" are children!

For me, fatherhood has been an unexpected adventure. As I told you, it was an experience for which I was largely unprepared. Even so, it has been a time that has held much delight and many satisfactions, accompanied, of course, by a few disappointments, bitter moments, and frustrations.

I wish that I had known twenty-one years ago what I know now about parenting and about the male role within parenting. There are some things I would have done much differently, and there are some things I did that I would have emphasized much more.

Permit me to share with you a personal pilgrimage about the changing role of father and some issues that are emerging in my new male consciousness. With parenthood as with all other roles there's a great deal of latitude, and so I'm not prescribing this as the only way for a father to perform his role. I simply offer some of my own discoveries to stimulate your thinking about what you want to be as father.

Escape from Traditional Assumptions

Escape from the assumption that "fathers don't have it . . . mothers are all."

How free we fathers could be if we could escape the widespread feeling that fatherhood is a secondary and inferior role to motherhood! "Fathers don't make good mothers" is what a family court judge said in 1975 when he denied a father's petition for custody of his preschool son.[1] The judge was merely echoing what had been assumed in family law and proclaimed by most social scientists—that mother is all-important to the child. Therefore, they implied that father is an inferior, minimally important partner in child rearing.

Social scientists have quite accurately and carefully observed the impact of mother's care on the child. They have seen the devastating effects of deprivation of that mother's attention. However, they have not gone on to ask, "Could a father have filled the void for a child deprived of a mother?"

Fortunately, the role of father is being reconsidered. Mary C. Howell, assistant professor of pediatrics at Harvard Medical School (herself the mother of six) suggests,

> The near-exclusive assignment of functional parenting to women is a condition of our society that is not universally shared by all human societies, nor even by all primate groups. We should, therefore, remember that the childcare usually performed by mothers might be just as well carried out by fathers.[2]

In our society it seems to be commonly assumed that women have a "maternal instinct." It is not assumed that men have a "parenting instinct" as well. We socialize women for the parenting role, but not men, and thus reinforce our own prejudice against significant male involvement in parenting.

A few recent studies are now revealing the tender parenting qualities of many fathers. For example, in a study at a Cincinnati hospital, fathers and mothers were given an equal opportunity to hold their babies during the first few days after birth. Surprise! Fathers were more likely than mothers to want to hold and look at their babies. James Levine comments, "At a time when such studies are rare, some researchers make it sound as if they had discovered a new creature—it doesn't lactate and it doesn't have a uterus, but it shows a surprisingly warm response to its offspring!''[3]

Drs. Martin Greenberg and Norman Morris have this to say about fathers' reactions to two- and three-day-old infants:

> The fathers enjoy looking at their babies as opposed to other babies and perceive the newborn to be attractive, or pretty, or beautiful. . . . There is a desire for and pleasure of tactile contact with the newborn. . . . Many of the fathers have reported themselves to be so moved by the impact of the newborn that they feel drawn in toward the baby as if it were a magnet. Their attraction to the newborn is very powerful, and it appears to be something over which they have no control. They do not will it to happen; it just does.[4]

This was my experience; when my children were born, I was drawn to them, pulled by a magnetic fascination much stronger that I had anticipated.

Levine suggests that perhaps current child-bearing practices (such as hospital procedures that don't allow fathers to be with their newly born infants) and cultural views which consider it unmanly for a man to have a tender interest in children are impairing the responsiveness that men could have to their children.

An infrequent but growing phenomenon reveals how strong a male's love of parenting can be. In July, 1965, the Boys' and Girls' Aid Society of Oregon placed an eighteen-month-old boy with a thirty-eight-year-old piano teacher and musician named Tony Piazza. This was the first adoption in the country by a single man.[5] When a national news service picked up the story, a powerful force was released. Men who had long cherished the same hope knocked on the doors of adoption agencies around the country with newspaper clippings in hand about the Piazza adoption. As single-parent adoptions continue to grow, a small minority of these have a man as the single parent. It is still a field where a man may expect resistance and prejudicial treatment. Still, those men who have adopted a child, and are successfully parenting that child, model for us all how strong the male's parenting desires and bonds can be.

Tony and all the others who eagerly pursue the single-parent adoptive-father role reinforce a powerful message to us: Fathering/nurturing is a deep drive for many of us men. This should be freely recognized and acted upon for all who feel it.

Not all men have equal interest in deep involvement in nurturing their children. Nor do all women. But for those who want to be more deeply involved, it is tragic to be hindered by a society's assumption that neither recognizes nor encourages the great contribution men can and do make to parenting.

Escape from the assumption that everything else is more important than parenting for a man.

A man faces a second problem if he wants to be a good father. Not only does he live with uncertainty about the importance of his part in parenting, he lives with many pressures which compete for the time that he might devote to fathering.

I guess I never felt disapproval for wanting to emphasize my fathering, but I did experience tremendous pressures from within and without to put my career ahead of everything else. Heavy job demands—day and night—meant that sometimes I wasn't there when my children needed me. Too often I missed the quiet enjoyment of our ending the day together. Occasionally either they or I looked in vain for the opportunity to say something sensitive or important to the other. Sometimes when their late announcements about events in which they were participating conflicted with work promises I had already made, I kept those work promises.

I still remember vividly the day we brought our first child home from the hospital. The hospital was one in which the father was not allowed near the child. I remember the wonder, the awe, the delight I felt as I held her and rocked her for the first time. This ecstasy lasted for twenty minutes, and then I had to leave to conduct—of all things—a children's activity at the church which employed me. At that point it had not occurred to me to find a substitute or cancel the activity for a week. I did not want to let go of my baby daughter, although there were others waiting their turn to hold her. But my mother-in-law said to me, "Don't worry, Dick. There will be plenty of time for this." Eighteen years later when I drove her to her college dormitory I wondered where that time had gone that I had been promised. The answer, I fear, was that too often I had not taken the time. No one could set my priorities other than I.

I was not alone in this battle of time. One person recalls of his father, "Dad mostly packed and unpacked." A writer describes the suburban father as merely a "boarder with sex privileges." Dr. Urie Bronfenbrenner tells of a study carried on by a team of researchers to learn how much time middle-class fathers spend with their children. The researchers first asked a number of fathers how much time they estimated that they spent interacting with their one-year-old children each day. The average answer was fifteen to twenty minutes. Then, to check the accuracy of this estimate, they attached microphones to the clothing of these small children to record actual parent-child conversation. They discovered that the average amount of time spent by those fathers with their small children was thirty-seven seconds per day! The recordings revealed that "their direct interaction was limited to 2.7 encounters daily, lasting ten to fifteen seconds each! That, so it seems, represents the contribution of fatherhood for millions of America's children." [6]

If we men are not available to our children due to time pressures to which we have yielded, how do our daughters learn to relate to men? How do our sons learn to be men? The answer, it seems, is that the sons learn masculinity from trial and error, their mothers, and their peers.

Ruth Hartley points out that in the absence of father young males do most of the learning about maleness from boys their own age and from the slightly older boys. There is a big problem with this; the boys from whom he learns have no better sources of information than he has. Therefore, all they can do is combine their impressions, anxieties, ignorance, and childish or youthful perceptions. [7] The father who yields to time pressures and becomes an absentee father is probably turning the raising of his children over to other children. This is particularly true in regard to his sons. The most important gift a man can give his children is solid presence, time, interest, friendship, and modeling of what it means to be an adult male.

Some men are challenging this time bind constriction on parenting in striking ways. Consider the following examples:

In 1971, Gary Ackerman, an elementary school teacher in New York City applied for a leave of absence so that he could stay at home and care for his infant daughter. The New York City Board of Education rejected his request. They responded that they gave maternity leaves but not paternity leaves. After two years of court battles, a ruling by the Federal Equal Employment Opportunity Commission in Ackerman's favor brought about a new policy in the school system: "maternity" leave policies are now available to either parent. [8] While this possibility does not seem to be widely utilized by men, some men are seeking ways to make time available so that they may take a larger, more active role in the parenting process.

Some fathers are negotiating for a shorter time at work so that they can take more fathering responsibilities and opportunities with their children. While there are new employment agencies attempting to place persons on twenty-five-hour work weeks, these agencies so far have been much more successful in placing women than men. Somehow employers can understand if a woman needs to work shorter hours in order to be able to devote time to a child. The same employers find it more difficult to comprehend why a man would want such time. Still, some men are finding ways to blaze a trail here. Levine tells of Eric Barrett, an executive for the educational division of a large national corporation. Eric requested a three-day work week so that he could have more time with his son, Tony, and so that his wife, Pam, could pursue a part-time career as a commercial artist. Apparently Eric was so valuable an employee that his boss allowed it.[9]

Then there are Steve and Debbie Hoffman, co-owners and operators of a Manhattan printing business. The Hoffmans share their work and the care of Michael, their two-year-old son. They do this by having one person at the office all the time and keeping one another totally informed about all aspects of the work.[10]

At Hampshire College each partner in several faculty couples has a half-time appointment, freeing the couple to share child care and home life and to pursue other vital interests.

Still other men, after consulting with their spouses about the best child-care options, have chosen yet another way—that of the man becoming a ''househusband'' or a ''father/homemaker.'' That is, the wife earns the family income and the husband provides management of the household and primary care for the children. Again, this is by no means an easy role to choose. While it may have much logic and fulfillment for the couple themselves, the role of homemaker has been given little prestige value by society. Society gives this role little value when a wife does it and even less when a husband chooses to do it! But some persons who are willing to risk not being understood still choose this life-style. For example, Jim Carter (no relationship to the former president) resigned his position as sales manager for a life insurance company to care for his children and provide day care for some other neighborhood children, a task he has discovered he much prefers. Or there is Phil Kramer, an attorney who, for a few years at least, will care for his daughter while his wife continues in her career as an educator so that he and his wife may raise her in the philosophy in which they believe.[11] For some homemaker fathers this may be a short-range decision; for others it may be longer lasting. When some couples find the need to give more time and attention to their children, occasionally they discover it makes more sense for the father to provide this attention.

Most fathers will find themselves in a three way tug-of-war for their time and energy: work versus family versus all the other interests and needs of their lives. In determining how to resolve that tug-of-war these fathers should become aware of how important—or unimportant—fathering is to them, and how brief a time they have for active involvement in the lives of their children. If they begin with conscious awareness of both of those factors, perhaps they will not fall into the trap of assuming that everything else is more important than parenting until the parenting opportunity is past.

Escape from the assumption that father must be "the heavy" or that father must be a "peer-pal."

One of the traditional characteristics of the male role, man as the aggressor, the violent one, the punisher, comes into play in fatherhood. Some of us grow up with the pattern that though father may not be home much, he is indeed the enforcer, the punisher. "Just wait until your father gets home; we'll see about that. . . ." Father's strength, his temper, his physical power, his aggressiveness, his final word—these are father as "the heavy." Certainly it is rare when this is a man's *only* role with his children, but in some instances, it is the dominating theme in a man's family involvement.

At the other extreme, some parents feel at a loss to communicate any standards, expectations, or discipline to their children. One frustrated father told me "I was raised to respect my elders. When I am an elder, it seems I am supposed to respect the wishes of my children."

Or, as another father said, "When I say no, my children don't like me," and the pain of not being liked caused him to say no very seldom, probably less than he felt he should.

Parenting according to the wishes of the children, according to the majority judgment of other parents, or according to the expert of the moment is apt to be confusing for the child and frustrating for the parent.

I call this lack of leadership the "peer-pal" style of fathering. Of course, I am not arguing against a deep sense of friendship between a father and his children. I am arguing against needing approval from children so badly that a man abdicates his place of parental leadership.

Escape from the Robert Young or the Dagwood Bumstead image.

Do you remember a TV series entitled "Father Knows Best" which starred Robert Young? For its day it was a fun and constructive program, communicating a joyful view of family living. However, the title summed up one of the major themes of the traditional male role—the solid, wise, compassionate, patient father who "knows best." When you think of it, the theme "Father knows best" is the extension of the "Sturdy Oak" concept of the male role into parenting. And it is just as unrealistic there as it is in other areas of a man's life. It is one thing for a man to want to give his best support to his children. It is another thing to hold an impossible standard in which father never blows his top, never makes mistakes, never fails, never is confused or has needs. This expectation is not realistic, and it is not healthy.

But more frequently, there is another "father image" portrayed in entertainment media: the Dagwood Bumstead, the lovable, inept buffoon. He is the father who is tolerated and laughed at but not respected. He is the powerless father. As the plaque in one kitchen put it: "The opinions expressed by the husband in this household are not necessarily those of the management." Beneath a rather thin veneer of humor, the message about these fathers is that they really don't know anything about parenting—that's woman's domain—but being men, they have to pretend they do. Poor, deceived, lovable, laughable oafs.

Such are some of the themes, assumptions, and images that exist about fatherhood in our society. Together they make a confused set, reflecting widespread uncertainty about what fathers are meant to be.

I'd like now to explore the directions that the new role of father might take.

Journey Toward a New Role as Father

Journey toward an integrated life. When it comes to managing time, most of us are like an overambitious juggler who tries to keep in circulation more balls than he can handle; he winds up dropping one or two, or maybe all of them. The constant danger that hard-driving, high-achieving men live with is that, in successfully circulating the ball called work, they drop the ball called parenting.

If a man is serious about his fathering, he will need to face the tension that the demands of work and the demands of fathering place on him. When he works unrealistic hours, he should recognize the convenient rationalization that "I am really doing it for them." His question needs to be, "Do they need the additional income more than they need me?"

I remember a time when I made a time decision in favor of fathering—for once. It was my middle daughter Lisa's senior year, and she played varsity basketball, an interest we had enjoyed in many a "one-on-one" game in our driveway. I determined that this was an unrepeatable opportunity to share with her the experiences of this last season of basketball. I decided I would be her number one fan. I determined not to miss a home game if possible. Once in a while I watched her instead of doing my work, and surprise! Things did not fall apart. Her last game came on the night of my official church board meeting, but I excused myself to go to her game. Lisa's team fooled me; they won in the last second, and so had another "last game" to play. What a thrilling moment of celebration with her I would have missed if I had not been there! That season stands out in my mind as one of the few right decisions I made about time and parenting. You readers who are younger parents are urged to think through what you would really like to share with your children. Then, I urge you, give that time priority. *Journey toward inner-directedness in my children.* The wise parent will both enjoy the process of being a parent and look at what the goal of parenting is. The goal is that when a child reaches age eighteen, he or she is ready for independent living. She or he will quite probably move into a dormitory, or barracks, or apartment. The eighteen-year-old will have to be ready to arrange a schedule, take initiative, manage money, and also be ready to choose and live out a life-style from the incredible variety of choices that are probably available on the same floor of that dormitory/barracks/apartment!

This goal suggests a way of parenting that is not unconscious imitation or rejection of the way you yourself were raised. Instead, it requires conscious, intentional parenting. Preparing the child to be an adult is the fitting style for today.

Parents need to give clear leadership about the self-disciplined life and then give children increasing freedom to try out the skills that they will need to be successful adults. This may suggest that as children move into their teens, you give them a larger allowance and let them budget their lunches and some clothing. It may suggest letting them set their own schedules so long as they get enough sleep to stay healthy. It may suggest letting them make their own decisions about school work so long as performance stays at a level acceptable both to the child and you. And it suggests stopping once in a while to evaluate the experience to see what you have learned and what needs to be changed.

Neither withdrawing from parental leadership nor total domination of children is suggested. Rather, clear, moral leadership by parents is important so that the child-becoming-an-adult is helped to take ever-increasing responsibility, so that the responsibilities of adult living do not come as a shock.

Journey toward providing nonsexist role expectations for children. If I recognize how dissatisfied I am with sex-role expectations for me as a male, then even more do I want to change the expectations that are passed on to my children. As I become disenchanted with the way things are, I begin to form a vision of a truly free world, where each person is free to be all that she or he wants to be, free of all the old limitations and stereotypes that have bound us in. As best I can, I want to journey toward building a small piece of that world in my home with my children.

For one thing, I will rid myself of preferring children of one sex or the other. I will avoid the stereotyped hope that first we will have a boy for me and then a girl for my wife. I will escape that age-old preference for male offspring.

Further, I will respond to their interests in a manner free of sex-role expectations. I will allow and encourage my sons to be tender and emotional, and I will allow and encourage my daughters to be independent and assertive. I will encourage both sons and daughters to be tender, emotional, and caring, as well as independent, assertive, and aggressive. Any toy, any hobby, any pursuit, any subject will be available to boys and girls without old sex-role constraints. I will respond to them as individuals, enjoy their individuality, encourage it.

As I become increasingly aware of sex-role binds that I am battling, I will both model a new style for my children and talk with them about the role stereotypes I am trying to change.

Letty Cottin Pogrebin has written a book on this subject, entitled *Growing Up Free: Raising Your Child in the 80's.*[12] In this carefully researched, well-thought-out book, she speaks both of the ideals that must be clarified and of the numerous influences that must be challenged and changed (within one's household and without) if nonsexist child rearing is actually to be accomplished. She speaks of five main objectives for nonsexist childrearing.

1. Achievement is a sex-neutral human need. All children should feel free to excel in any field and to enjoy fully the fruits of their performance.
. . .

2. Success is sexless. Parents should help both girls and boys strive freely, take pride in their accomplishments, and be realistic about their failures.
. . .

3. Children should be able to accept and enjoy the bodies they were born with and should not compromise their health to satisfy the dictates of an ideal "image". . . .

4. Girls and boys should be encouraged to express themselves with originality and enthusiasm, however iconoclastic their interests—and to make independent judgments based on facts, feelings, logic, pleasure, and consideration for others, without regard for sex-role "propriety". . . .

5. Children and adults alike should throw off "the curse of the ideal" and the burden of emotional self-censorship—and should reach beyond the cliches of gender to discover who we are, what we really feel, and how happy we can be. . . .[13]

If one accepts these goals, a great deal of changed behavior as a parent will need to follow. But the struggle will be worth the effort, for it is within our homes that the gentle revolution of which we have been speaking can begin to happen.

Journey toward communicating more thoroughly one's beliefs, values, and commitment. Certainly one of the most important gifts I can give my children is a clear communication of my faith commitment. I know I cannot pass it on automatically. I know that they must question it, test it, perhaps abandon it for a while, before they can decide for themselves. Still, they deserve to know in what I believe and how life makes sense and has meaning for me. They need to know my values and morals and why I hold them.

However, much gets in the way of this kind of communication between a parent and children. Providing for food, housing, clothing, education, medical care; making decisions about schedules, lessons, allowances; chauffering; making decisions about all the questions and requests put to us—all tend to consume the available family time. However, we are communicating beliefs and values within all those decisions. And then, too, somehow we parents fear imposing our beliefs on our children. We tend to wait until they ask us. But what if they never ask?

How much better it would be to have values discussions carried on in a spirit of free dialogue and discovery: "Here's what I believe about friendships, or pressures, or white lies, or cheating. . . . What do you believe?" In Deuteronomy 6:7, after we are commanded to love the one God with all our heart, soul, and might, the passage continues:

And these words which I command you this day shall be upon your heart; and you shall teach them diligently to your children, and shall talk of them when you sit in your house, and when you walk by the way, and when you lie down, and when you rise . . . (Deuteronomy 6:6-7).

In this ancient command, there is much we have ignored. In rethinking parenthood we can try to embody the guidance from this verse.

Journey toward contributing to my children's vocational decisions. Parents have an unfortunate tendency to feel that they have little or nothing to offer their children in making decisions about vocation, work, and career. Fewer and fewer children follow their parents into the same occupation. Increasingly, the terminology and content of children's school work changes so that parents feel ineffective when they try to help. The world of work offers more and more complex choices.

Parents tend to feel uninformed and helpless. Thus, they leave the vocational guidance of their children to others. The "others" may include an overloaded school counselor who knows little about the young person and his or her interests and strengths.

We can do better than that. Parents have more to offer their children in this area than they may believe. Consider these findings of leading vocational psychologists:

—A vocational choice is an expression of who you are (and who knows better what a child is good at or what a child feels is important than the parent—and the child, of course).

—The most accurate predictor of success in work is the answer to these questions: "Do I like it? Do I enjoy it?" (Again, the child and parents know the answer better than anyone else).

—Many vocational choices are made on the basis of wanting to imitate some "model," some person the child admires.

The parent has rich opportunities from early childhood on to help the child gain information for vocational choices. A parent can take the child to work with him or her from time to time so that the child has firsthand knowledge about what work father or mother does. The child will have opportunity also to see what other work associates do.

A parent can introduce a child to other persons whose career might interest the child. For example, my children have been enriched by meeting gifted Christian artists (music, drama, clowning, photography, painting) who came to provide leadership for our church. Each of these artists was so generous with time and concern for the young people who shared their interests that whole new worlds opened up before them.

When doing family work with the child, the parent can model and expect of the child good work habits. Those work habits of responsibility, reliability, and punctuality can, in themselves, carry one far in the world of work.

When the child becomes youth or young adult, the parent can help find work opportunities—either volunteer or paid—that may help the young person participate in and investigate work activities that hold possible interest. While still a high school student, one of my children found the oppportunity to investigate a possible vocational interest. During a two-week interim program at her school, she arranged to spend eight hours a day in the public relations department of a local corporation, experiencing one way that her journalistic interests could be used. This was made possible by the generous help of the person who headed that department, someone we knew from our church. Whether my child becomes a journalist or not, she has some important vocational information she could have gained in no other way.

A parent can offer to be listener and helper when the young person needs to make those decisions about what to do after high school. Such decisions may well seem awesome and overwhelming since the days after graduation are the very first not planned by someone else. However, the sensitive parent can be of help. While not taking away the young adult child's freedom to decide, the parent can help him or her ask the right questions and explore the answers. The young adult is apt to think she or he needs to make decisions about a whole lifetime, when rather she or he needs to make basic decisions for the next year or so. Among those decisions are:

—What do I need right now? (work experience? some distance from my family for a while? a chance to investigate some possible careers? the opportunity to continue my education?)

—What steps can I take to accomplish the things I need to do right now?

For some parents this may mean visiting and investigating colleges with their young adult child. Together they can investigate the question, "Does this college fit the person?" Does it offer good programs in his or her fields of interest? Is it affordable? And then the partnership in planning college finances can begin.

For other parents it may mean a patient, sometimes painful, wait while the young adult does a lot more sorting out. During these years the parent walks the thin line between being dominator and being abdicator. But this thin line can lead to a good place, a place where one can be friend and consultant to one's adult children while trusting them with the integrity of all their decisions.

Finally, take some miscellaneous journeys. Out of the joys and regrets of parenting I share with you a few more observations.

I wish I had spent more time with *each child individually*. I remember a time when we were vacationing within an hour's drive of the Pro Football Hall of Fame. I announced to my family I'd like to go to see it and invited them to come. Only my middle child, then eight years old, wanted to go. As we drove toward the museum, she looked over at me and said, "I've been dreaming of this for a long time, Dad." "What's that, honey?" I asked. "Just you and me doing something all by ourselves for a whole day," she responded. I was astounded. I did not realize how much a shared activity for just the two of us would mean to each one. I tried to learn from that experience and look for opportunities to do something with one child at a time—from going out to dinner to taking one with me on a trip to a convention, from overnight bike hikes to afternoon outings. So much joy, love, and influence, so many secrets and dreams, can be shared one on one. I wish I had done more of that.

I would also create more family rituals. Some of these rituals would be explicitly religious; others would simply celebrate a person or the whole family. We have created some rituals unique for our family. For a number of years when my children were small, we created our own little Christmas pageant for their mother and any other Christmas guests.

We also have special ways of celebrating birthdays, baptisms, graduations. But a family in touch with its faith heritage can build rituals that are uniquely its own and a part of the bonds of the family.

One thing I would do exactly as we did. We were committed to our children's total growth, learning, discovery, development. Within the limits of our ability to pay, we provided opportunities for lessons, musical instruments, learning or camp opportunities. We felt no compulsion that children must continue everything they began. They had the right to discover what they loved or enjoyed, where they excelled, and where they did not.

There is one widely read family life expert who proclaims that lack of firm discipline is the greatest family illness today.[14] That was not our experience. We happened on to a style of discipline that was right for our family. As I look back, it looks something like this. Whenever possible, we consulted on discipline matters. When it was not possible to consult, both parents stood behind the decision either made. We had a very small core of absolutely firm parental expectations. First wc tried various ways of influencing our children to fulfill these expectations, but when all else failed, we demanded this fulfillment. That core decreased as they grew older, the goal being their own inner-disciplined lives.

One thing I would occasionally do differently. I sometimes fell into some teasing or "kidding" of my children, which unknowingly hurt them. I failed to realize how powerful parents are. What I intended as harmless teasing did not feel so to my children at times. I failed to realize that as long as children are among siblings and peers, they will have plenty of people to keep them humble through teasing. My play and humor with them could have been more affirming and upbuilding.

I would lobby with the church of which I am a part to do more things in which the whole family could participate together. Some of our family's rich memories come from such church activities that we all enjoyed—an intergenerational choir, family camp, all-church retreats, special celebrations, guest artists at the church. The range of experiences that the church could offer to families would be much richer if the church leaders would use imagination and the rich resources available.

In Conclusion

I am advocating that men find a new emphasis on fatherhood as they renegotiate their roles. The new world of awareness, freedom, and relationships that they envision should be tried out experimentally with their children and communicated to them. Though there will be little societal support for this emphasis on the father as parent (except from

your children and other parents who feel the same way), I am convinced
that fatherhood is an opportunity for a richer life and a deeper influence
on others than any other available to a man.

The writer to Ephesians counsels us, "Fathers, do not provoke your
children to anger, but bring them up in the discipline and instruction
of the Lord." And in another connection, speaking of all human relationships, the writer continues, ". . . and be kind to one another,
tenderhearted, forgiving one another, as God in Christ forgave you"
(Ephesians 6:4; 4:32). The father who parents in the light of those
verses is the different kind of person who just may help a new kind of
world to dawn.

9

You Don't Own Her Anymore

Changing Marriage

We have been discussing marriage-related issues through most of what we have already explored. We spoke of men becoming more aware of and expressing their emotions; we spoke of men developing a greater capacity for friendship; we spoke of greater freedom and expressiveness in our sexuality; we spoke of the losses and gains in the human-liberation movement; we spoke of role-free parenting. In each instance we were speaking about matters that can have an impact on one's marriage.

I'm not unaware of the issues and problems of the many single men. I hope that those single men sense that the earlier chapters which urge a man to get in touch with his attitude toward his role, his emotions and his relational skills have value for building a meaningful life-style as a single. The male reader may not be married, and he may not be a father. But since these are two areas that are deeply impacted by the changing male/female roles, I hope that the single or childless reader has indulged me as I have looked at parenting and will indulge me as I now examine marriage.

Now we look directly at marriage. What shape will marriage take when role expectations change?

Perhaps we can best begin to answer that by looking at the shape marriage has had in the past. Letha and John Scanzoni point out, in regard to the sharing of influence or power, there are four possible types:

a) the owner-property type. The husband owns all, perhaps even "owns" people, including his wife. He, therefore, has absolute power and his wife has none.

b) the head-complement type. Here, the husband has by far the vast majority of the power, and his wife has a little authority.

c) the senior-junior partnership type. In this type of marriage the husband has most of the power, but the wife is granted a significant percentage of it.

d) the equal-partnership type. Power is fluid; it may be shared equally by the marriage partners or may flow appropriately from one to the other.

As the Scanzonis point out, until this century the owner-property type of marriage was almost universal. "A person's power over another person depends on the resources he or she holds out to that person, how dependent that second person is on these resources, and whether or not that second person can find alternate sources for the benefits elsewhere." [1] In other words, if a woman's choice is either to submit to that kind of autocratic authority or to starve to death, probably her survival instincts will prevail. Now with increased economic opportunities for women, quite likely the pattern of marriage is changing quickly and abruptly.

What Does the Bible Say?

At this point the reader may be wondering, "Doesn't the Bible command that marriage be structured with the husband as the head, the dominant authority?" For a marriage to be biblically based, does it not need to be of the owner-property type, or at least head-complement or senior-junior partnership type? Would not an equal-partnership type marriage be contrary to the teaching of Scripture? Regardless of how economics and work patterns may change, is not that the way the Bible teaches that marriage ought to be?

There are many books on Christian marriage on the market now that would have you think so. The husband is the dogmatic authority (benevolent and kindly, perhaps, but the final authority nevertheless). The wife is the subservient one. She may be able to disguise this cleverly, if she is adoring enough, flattering enough, sexy enough for her husband. But he is her master, her lord—so much so that Virginia Ramey Mollenkott sees idolatry in some of these books. Mollenkott points out that the woman is urged virtually to worship her husband. [2] This pattern is urged in such books, it is said, because this is what the Bible teaches. *Is it really?*

I do not think so. As a matter of fact, such books represent a rather tragic misreading of the Bible, in my opinion.

In order to examine the Bible's teaching on marriage, let's recall the Bible study principles that we suggested in chapter 3. I suggested four

Bible-study principles: *(a)* we should not absolutize the culture in which a Bible passage was written; *(b)* in reading a Bible passage we should carefully discern between the cultural assumptions and the explicit biblical teaching; *(c)* we should begin with the major Bible themes, doctrines, commands; *(d)* we should use the life, behavior, and teachings of Jesus Christ to provide specific guidance.

Let's apply these principles in looking at Ephesians 5:21-33, one of the most complete statements on marriage between partners who are both Christians.

Bible scholars are discovering that for a long time translators were dividing paragraphs at the wrong place. (There were no paragraphs in the original text). Thus the paragraph we are discussing should not begin at verse 22, "Wives be subject to your husbands. . . ." but at verse 21 "Be subject to one another out of reverence for Christ." As a matter of fact, there is no verb in verse 22; it is simply implied from verse 21. The rather literal rendering of verses 21-22 would be, "Being subject to one another in the fear of Christ, wives to their own husbands as to the Lord."[3] This passage then does not merely teach wifely submission; what it teaches instead is *mutual submission.*

The writer goes on to tell wives to relate to their husbands as the church does to Jesus Christ. "Wives, be subject . . . as to the Lord" (5:22). That is, with the same joy, eagerness, and love that the church is to have for Christ (verses 23-24).

But then the passage goes on to give even more delicate and detailed instructions to husbands. They are to love their wives "as Christ loved the church and gave himself up for her" (5:25). Remember that was a sacrifice of his very life. (A description of Christ's giving of himself for the church is found in Philippians 2:3-8.) The husband should be concerned for his wife's greatest welfare and maximum participation in their holy union. Further, the husband should love his wife as he loves his own body. And we provide for our body's pleasure and the avoidance of pain quite regularly, don't we? "For no man ever hates his own flesh, but nourishes it and cherishes it . . ." (Ephesians 5:29*a*). The husband is to recall those great verses from the story of creation that man and woman are created for each other: ". . . a man shall leave his father and mother and be joined to his wife and the two shall become one flesh" (5:31). In this passage Paul has clearly prescribed a submissive love for husbands as well as wives. "The Christian way of relating is *mutual* submission, and *mutual* service, and *mutual* love."[4] The conclusion of Paul's advice to husbands and wives is, "let each one of you love his wife as himself, and let his wife see that she respects her husband" (5:33).

The first readers of these words might have come from Roman, or Greek, or Hebrew cultures. In each of those cultures the husband had a position of unquestioned dominance, privilege, and authority. Men had the privileges; women had none. And so the first readers of these words would have been astounded! They would rightly have sensed that if one suggested that marriage was to be compared to the love between Christ and church, or if one suggested that marriage was to be marked by mutual submission—well, that was nothing less than revolutionary!

And so we must read these words not only for what they say, but for the direction in which they point. This direction reveals a marriage in which each partner is respected, a marriage in which the unique gifts of each are claimed and used. There is no assumption that one partner is always right. No one is more important. No one is necessarily superior spiritually. No one should always have the last word. Mutual submission means that each partner is concerned for the happiness and self-esteem of the other.

Richard D. Kahoe has conducted studies that show that it is psychologically unhealthy for both women and men to favor female subordination. A woman who is always submissive to men may be "self-protective, risk-avoiding, resistant to change, and maladjusted. 'Men who oppose equality for women tend to be more authoritarian and nonconforming, higher in general neuroticism and need for power, and less reflective and self-reliant.'"[5]

I would contend that the Bible (Ephesians 5:21-33, in particular) points the way for couples to develop a marriage style that may be quite different from that of other couples. The decisions made in this freeing marriage style will be determined by the answers to four questions: *(a)* What is good for me? *(b)* What is good for my partner? *(c)* What is good for our relationship? *(d)* How can we keep growing, individually and together? (After building a strong marriage, there is commitment to a wider community that must also be considered.)

Meanwhile, Back in the Twentieth Century—the Two-Career Marriage

The most predominant characteristic of changing marriage in our day is the increase of marriages in which both partners are employed outside the home. Carolyn Bird points out that though the image of the American family usually involved a homemaking mother, a breadwinning father, and a couple of dependents, by the late 1970s only 7 percent of married couples fit this pattern.[6] Nearly 60 percent of all wives were employed outside the home. (In addition there were the single-mother households, single fathers, etc.)

Bird interviewed hundreds of couples. She categorized them by the activity and attitude of the wife with regard to the wife's working outside the home. The couple's adjustment to the two-career marriage depended on which category the couple was in. Her classifications included:

1. Traditional homemakers. These women's husbands prefer that they stay at home, and they quite happily agree. They see marriage as a challenge that can utilize all the skills that the wife wishes to bring to it.

2. Defiant homemakers. The smallest group, they are women who insist on staying at home though their husbands want them to work. Many of these persons are from higher income brackets and so don't need the money. They feel that the children they raise or the other activities in which they are engaged are more satisfying than a job would be.

3. Submissive homemakers. These are women whose husbands want them to stay home, but they would prefer to go to work outside the home. These are persons who do not find homemaking satisfying and would love to enter the work force as a way of growing. For some reason they are prohibited from doing so. For example, wives of community leaders and politicians sometimes have to repress what they want to do for fear of the reflection it will cast on their husbands.

4. Reluctant homemakers. Bird describes these persons as the "two-time losers." These are women who want to be able to earn, and their husbands want them to, also. But there is something that holds them back, perhaps lack of training, perhaps competition for jobs, perhaps lack of opportunity in their fields of interest.

5. Reluctant working wives. These are women who would prefer not to work outside the home, and their husbands share that preference, but for some reason, often the shortage of enough money for the family to survive otherwise, they are gainfully employed outside the home.

6. Submissive working wives. Such women would prefer to quit and specialize in homemaking, but their husbands want them to keep working.

7. Defiant working wives. These women are working because they want to and choose to. Their husbands do not like it, but they stick by their decision. Bird notes that statistics reveal that nearly one working wife out of five thinks that her husband resents her working outside the home.

8. Contemporary working wives. These are the women who are working because that is what both they and their husbands want.[7]

It stands to reason that the couples in categories one and eight have the greatest possibility of some sort of marriage harmony. For persons in both of those categories the husband's preference, the wife's preference, and the circumstances of their lives all concur. Since category one is shrinking and category eight is growing, couples need to develop skills for developing meaningful marriage in that style.

When I asked one mental health counselor who had been in practice for many years what mental health strains he found in men due to the pressures of changing roles, he pointed to the two-career marriage. He pointed out that men whose marriages are two-career marriages, but who have assumptions from the one-career, traditional marriage (assumptions about male authority, decision making, distribution of money, rigid division of household work) were troubled in themselves and troubled in relationship to their wives.

The man who is able to recognize the subtle and not-so-subtle changes that two careers bring to marriage is apt to be the happier. This is especially so if he has the flexibility to learn to change role expectations in accordance with what he sees.

G. Wade and Mary Jo Rowatt were a married couple who moved from being a one-career to being a two-career couple. They wrote of their experience in their book, *The Two-Career Marriage*.[8]

The Rowatts, early in their marriage, discovered what they had failed to discuss before being married: that Wade did not want Jodi to work outside the home, but that she found it much more fulfilling to do so. And so, rather shortly, they became a two-career married couple.

While attempting to balance marriage, parenthood, and career, the Rowatts reported that they experienced several areas of stress and hurt. First, they had to face the question "Whose job has priority?"[9] Their first job offers were a thousand miles apart, and though Wade's field (ministry) might well have more widely available opportunities than Jodi's (music therapy), Wade accepted his position, and Jodi found herself without satisfying outlets in the career for which she was qualified. They feel their marriage suffered because of the conflict between their two-career needs. They reflect,

> We would perhaps move again if faced with a similar situation, but not as casually. Certainly we would discuss more fully our feelings, hopes, and personal goals. Neither of us would demand that the other move for a new position or stay because of our present job. Our dual-career marriage for a time had become a career duel![10]

A second area of hurt was implied in Wade's question, "Why isn't dinner ready?" Even if the wife works outside the home, is she expected to do all the traditionally assigned roles in the home as well?

This is a hotly debated issue on which there are strong feelings.

Consider a U.S. senator's statement, "I believe that women should be allowed to do anything they want to, as long as they are home in time to fix supper." Consider the equally strong statement I once saw on a woman's T shirt, "Women are expected to do twice as much as men. Fortunately, that's not difficult."

The Rowatts worked out a shared role, a shared duty system that was flexible within their own work schedules and capabilities. They recall, "Sharing domestic tasks wasn't as bad as getting used to the idea. The idea of shared home care violated ideals deeply ingrained by traditional culture." [11]

In regard to shared tasks in the home, a male friend of mine reported yet another experience. It seems that on his day off, Ron decided to spend the afternoon preparing a truly super supper for Marge when she came home from work—stuffed pork chops, baked potatoes, the best he could do. He anticipated their enjoying this meal together, and then relaxing together and enjoying each other for the evening.

Marge came in from her job as a YWCA executive somewhat tired and rushed. Immediately the phone rang for her, and she promised to go out that evening to respond to some matter that needed her attention.

As they sat down to eat, Ron was aware he was not feeling the delight he had anticipated; rather, he was feeling tightness and resentment within himself. Silently, he recalled that she had been gone on a work-related trip the previous week, and then tonight, when he had worked hard in the kitchen and had looked forward to being with her, she was leaving again. He sensed that in a very brief time he had fallen into a "taken-for-granted-househusband syndrome." Fortunately he was enough in touch with his feelings to recognize them and talk them out with Marge, so that they could work out an acceptable solution. The learnings Ron experienced both from his feelings during that supper and from his dealing with them were rich for him.

A third area of stress for the Rowatts was the shortage of time expressed in the cry "We just can't get it done tonight." "We felt like two clowns trying to perform simultaneously in three circus rings. We were tired, fatigued, and drained." [12] In time Wade and Jodi discovered how to modify habits and routines and reduce some of the expectations they had about house, lawn, and car. In such manner the tension over time decreased, but of course it did not disappear.

A fourth source of hurt came from their workaholic life-style that allowed little time for play, little time for each other, and little time for spiritual replenishment as individuals or as a couple. They discovered that while they could live off their heritage for a while, the need for relaxation, play, worship, and spiritual renewal could only be ignored at great peril to them both, as individuals and as a couple.

A fifth problem was their sense of isolation from acquaintances or friends. The press of time prohibited their planning leisurely dinner parties or other time-consuming entertaining of friends.

Sixth, there was stress from questions about child care and family demands. The key question was, "Whose children are these and who is responsible for their care?" They sensed that even though they both expressed responsibility for their children, the greater part of the burden fell on Jodi. Experiences shared by many employed couples reveals that their plans seem to include everything but a sick or injured child. That one additional strain on time of an emergency or illness is sometimes more than a couple can endure. [13]

The Rowatts discovered that the stress that comes to a marriage that is a two-career partnership is greatest in the first year and decreases (without disappearing) after that. They persisted in their two-career pattern because they found that it carried rewards sufficient to justify the difficulties encountered. These are some of the satisfactions and rewards they gained:

First, they benefited financially from two incomes. This greater financial base can give a greater freedom of choice about life-style, continuing education, or career change for either or both partners. They caution, however, that the increase in financial resources is never as much as it may appear. Higher tax brackets, transportation and child-care costs, and additional "farmed out" housework cut deeply into the extra resources provided by the two paychecks.

Second, they found that the family grows emotionally when both parents work. Once the need for close attachment to parents in young children is met, children may benefit from learning their responsible place in the family. It is discovered that children are more likely to help do the routine household work if parents are working. Children also have two models as they think about and plan their careers and marriages. Parents have benefits, too. Their satisfactions are spread broadly among marriage, parenthood, work, and other interests. Thus parents may be more ready for the "empty nest" period of their lives. The Rowatts believe that generally satisfaction with marriage is higher for dual-career couples.

A third benefit they discovered was in the area of experienced freedom. The wife experiences personal freedom in obtaining a job and doing it well. The social interaction with other adults at work is also a freedom gain. A freedom from role expectations—defining what is proper for a man and what is proper for a woman to do in the home—

also can develop. Thus, both marriage partners become more adaptable and more able to deal with crises as they occur.

A fourth benefit to which the Rowatts point is the growth options that are available to each. Employment may well be a source of personal growth and satisfaction. A woman may experience personal fulfillment from the contribution she makes through her work. A man may grow from increased involvement in the parenting activities with his children. The Rowatts felt that these benefits of a two-career marriage outweighed the hazards, once a reasonable balance between employment and home was achieved and once some of the more frantic, compulsive aspects of domestic homemaking were let go.[14]

Francine and Douglas Hall are also a two-career couple who have done considerable investigation about this new pattern of marriage. Out of their research they developed a number of hypotheses about what elements make two-career couples more apt to be compatible and successful. They suggest: "Two careers are more likely to be compatible if one partner ranks career number one and the other ranks family number one . . . or if both rank family number one . . . than if both partners give career top priority." Further, "Two careers are more likely to be compatible if both partners are in similar fields." Not everyone agrees with them on this one. However, they contend that when the partners know each other's work, they can be more understanding and supportive.

Further still, "Two careers are more likely to be compatible if there are no children." They find that it is relatively easy to juggle two roles (career and spouse). But when the third role (parent) is added, independence and flexibility are reduced.

They suggest also, "Two careers are more likely to be compatible if they are in different stages than if they are in the same stage," the same career stage, that is. They point out that each of us goes through a variety of career stages: *(a)* finding a career and obtaining a job in that career; *(b)* getting established and advancing in that career; *(c)* maintaining oneself and contributing to that career from the point of advancement. They suggest that couples who are not in the same stage at the same time may be more compatible. However, they find room for disagreement on this one, also.

Also, "Two careers are likely to be compatible when the two jobs . . . allow autonomy and flexibility." If there is some privilege of choosing one's hours, when and where one does one's work, then some of the family crises (such as a child's sickness) that arise in all families can be much better managed. For example, the Halls are both university educators, and thus have a certain flexibility of schedule. One of them can sometimes work at home if needed.

And finally, "Two careers are more likely to be compatible if the partners are mutually supportive, skilled at problem solving, and committed to each other's career." [15] They remind us that a two-career relationship is made of up to five ingredients: "two careers; two independent people, and one relationship. In our enthusiasm for developing the first four, let's not crowd out the fifth." [16] The Halls point to a key issue. Just as spouses sometimes neglect each other because of overemphasis on parenting, so can they neglect each other because of overemphasis on career. There needs to be not only careful organization of a two-career marriage but also empathy, support, interest in each other, and intimacy. It takes much effort to keep a marriage going with all the time pressures of such a life-style. The marriage partners need to give to each other and ask of each other personal interest, care, and support. That will make the marriage worth the effort.

Or to Put It Another Way

During the time I was working on this project, a friend of ours hosted my family and me to a lovely evening out—dinner theatre featuring the Irving Berlin musical "Annie Get Your Gun." For the most part, the play was good fun with lots of nostalgia about old tunes I had almost forgotten. In this story a remarkably liberated and free-spirited Annie bumbles her way when she tries to relate to people (or more precisely, a person) she cares about. Then comes the climax, the punch line. Although she is the best sharpshooter in the world, she has to throw the match and concede that *he* is the best in the world, if she is to win the man she loves!

Is that just a 1940s musical about turn-of-the-century male mentalities? Can one just enjoy the music and ignore the story line, saying that such viewpoints are long past?

I'm afraid these attitudes are still very much with us. Some 1970s research revealed that 66 percent of the women surveyed believed that their husbands would not like it if the wife was promoted to a better job than her husband. However, only 29 percent of the women thought that their husbands would *express* those feelings. Thirty-eight percent of the women believed that their husbands would consider it a threat to their masculinity if their wives held a better job than they. But only 4 percent felt that their husbands would admit this. [17]

Just the day before I wrote this, the "Accent" section of my community's local daily newspaper had a feature article with this bold headline: "Some Husbands Aren't Threatened by Wife's Success."

That's news? Apparently the editor thought so. Actually, the story didn't deliver what the headline promised, for it described just *one* husband who was not threatened by his wife's success. She was doing fabulously in real estate, but he was so secure in himself and in his accomplishments as a business consultant that he could relax and be pleased by her success.[18]

There is no doubt that marriage is undergoing radical change. Can marriage and family life still be strong in the present and coming era? Yes, but as the pioneering couples we have quoted above point out: if marriage and family are to be strong, a new spirit of flexibility, openness, and willingness to experiment and make new commitments will need to be exerted. If men can let go of their "Sturdy Oak" image, the need to be the *only* person on whom others depend, and their "Big Wheel" image, the need to succeed more than others, then they can move into a new style of marriage that may well have more rewards for both partners.

10

Competitors, Colleagues, Bosses

Changing Work

A Personal Perspective

Some time ago, I received a letter in the mail from the leader of a department of my denomination, a person of my acquaintance. His letter announced that he was looking for an associate to work with him. He wondered if I might be interested in applying. The letter made it clear that he was sending this announcement to a number of persons.

As I reflected on that letter, it began to occur to me that the opportunities of this position fit perfectly with my interests, my skills, and my dreams. I began to daydream about the job, about the chance to spend a good part of my time on the causes most dear to my heart, about the chance to influence not just one community but many communities across the nation, perhaps a whole denomination.

I became very excited about this position. I called the colleague who had sent me the letter. "I think I'd like to throw my hat in the ring," I told him. "Please consider me among the applicants to be your associate." There was a long silence on the other end, and then he said "Dick, I guess I sent those letters out prematurely. I'm under a good deal of pressure from my supervisors to hire a woman." And that was the last I heard of the matter except for the form letter announcing the name of the woman who was hired.

A few months later a friend called me with a "hot tip." A seminary of my denomination had decided to hire a new faculty member in the field of my specialty, social ethics. Since I had worked very hard to earn a doctorate in that field and since the opportunities to use it in the teaching ministry are very rare, this was exciting news indeed.

105

I called the president of that theological school, again a person of my acquaintance. He was very cordial, but told me I should apply to the dean. Since the dean had gone on an extended trip, he suggested that I apply in writing and send credentials to him. Needless to say, I did that right away.

After waiting a decent interval of time and hearing nothing, I called the dean to see if I could come talk to him. His answer was very frank and to the point, "If I can't get a black or a Hispanic, *then* I will look at your credentials," he said. And that was the end of it. He hired a man from Central America.

I experienced a good bit of anger over these two incidents. I felt that it was tough enough to get consideration for the specialized, difficult tasks for which I was qualified at this point in my career. I well knew that my field is crowded with highly qualified people, and I might well lose out in an open competition. But to see two "plums" dangled in front of my eyes and then to be ruled out of both, before the competition even began, because I was the wrong sex or the wrong ethnic group was a rather embittering experience.

For the first time in my life, I began to understand emotionally the issues of the Bakke case.* I could understand why a usually privileged white male would feel discrimination toward him. My sympathies switched from the discriminated-against minorities to the discriminated-against white Anglo-Saxon male. I discovered the limitations of my compassion; I was willing to give beleagured minority persons or women anything but first chance at a job I wanted! I'm not proud of all this, but that is exactly how I was feeling.

A couple years have passed since those experiences. Since then, I have left one significant job and accepted a new one. I have had a chance to do some thinking. Several things have occurred to me.

First, if society is in imbalance one way, giving preference to one group, it is going to have to be in imbalance the other way, giving preference to the opposite group, before things level off. The persons involved will probably always feel that the adjustments are unfair. To be truthful, I'd rather that these be worked out in the generations before me or after me. I'd like to be considered on my own merits. Still, we don't pick the age in which we live or the issues of our age. We simply live in that age, and participate in those issues.

*In 1977, Allen Bakke, a white male, filed suit arguing reverse discrimination. He had been denied admission to the University of California Davis Medical School, although he contended his scores were superior to minority persons who had been admitted under a quota system. The case went all the way to the United States Supreme Court, which ruled against the quota system.

Second, perhaps my best contribution can be to accept this process with as little bitterness as possible. Frankly, I'd rather be center stage in the battle for social justice, but it appears to me that in these and other cases I can give most by accepting the fact that it is someone else's turn for center stage. That's not easy for me to do, but sometimes it appears to be the right thing for this era.

Third, I need to recognize that where I am now is a place of profound male privilege. My last two jobs have had rather nice rewards in the way of recognition, esteem, affection, and decent financial compensation. I need to recognize that I was offered each of these two jobs not only because of my qualifications, but because I was a white male with these qualifications.

Fourth, I must confess what I never said to either committee that selected me. I never said, "Did you do a complete search? Are you sure that you have considered all of the possible qualified candidates including women, blacks, Hispanics? Did you consider highly qualified but aging persons?" I never said that. It never even occurred to me to say that.

Fifth, if I allow them to be so, the experiences which I described at the beginning of this chapter can be a valuable resource for me. I have had an opportunity to experience what women and minority persons experience many times over and to feel what they feel. This in turn can lead me to a closer identification with them and their issues.

Sixth, I have been stunned to put my rather minor gripe into perspective. Recently the following paragraph, a summary from the United Nations/World Conference on Women, which met in Copenhagen, Denmark, in July 1980, jumped out at me:

> Women are one-half of the world's population and one-third of the world's official work force, account for two-thirds of all working hours, receive one-tenth of the world's income, own less than one percent of the world's property, and constitute two-thirds of the world's illiterate. In an unequal world, women remain dependent, discriminated against, disadvantaged. Their contributions are undervalued and invisible, and they do not share in the benefits of development.[1]

To the extent that this information is accurate and true, my complaint really becomes quite trivial, even to me, the one most involved. As a Christian I feel called to care more about people, including people I will never know, who endure massive discrimination, than about myself when I endure minor discrimination.

I have shared some of my struggles and hurts in the workplace because I am quite sure that each reader is, or will be, undergoing changes in the work place as well. The form these issues take may be quite different for you than for me, but you will have to face them just as I had to face mine.

A Wider Perspective

There are many changes coming to the world of work. I must concentrate simply on the changes in regard to men and women in the marketplace.

For one thing, the number of women in the workforce employed outside the home is increasing dramatically. In the United States, in 1900, 5.6 percent of all married women were formally employed. In 1970, 40 percent of all married women had jobs, and by 1975, the number had increased to 50 percent![2]

For another thing, the women in the work force are being accepted in virtually all areas of occupational opportunity. There was a time when the women employed were largely segregated in a group of occupations that were somehow deemed "appropriate" for women. Elementary education, nursing, retail clerking, and secretarial services were among those occupations; each of these sadly carried low compensation. Concerning the women workers of a previous generation, Gilbert Chesterton quipped, "Twenty million young women rose to their feet with the cry, 'We will not be dictated to,' and promptly became stenographers."[3] But that is changing. The areas of work that are reserved solely for one sex are rapidly disappearing.

Women are seeking access to jobs on all levels of the work structure. They seek not just jobs, but good jobs. They, quite appropriately, want the opportunity to advance and to lead, just as men have access to these powers and privileges.

Finally, women are expecting equal pay for equal work. This is probably the most universally accepted goal of the feminist movement. This goal is one of necessity for many. Increasingly, in areas with a high cost of living, one income is not enough to provide for family needs. Single parent households headed by a woman are those which suffer most cruelly from the inequity of pay.

Part of the change in the world of work is that increasing numbers of men will experience women as competitors, colleagues, and even bosses. Let's take a look at each of these in turn.

Men and Women as Competitors with Each Other

A bright executive, age 29, who has had a number of rapid promotions, nonetheless resigns from a company and later takes a new and promising position. Is that so unusual? Is it newsworthy anyplace except on the business page of the newspaper published in the community where the business executive resigned? Is that a story that commands national attention in print, radio and television media?

The answer is yes, if the executive who resigned is Mary Cunningham, former vice president of strategic planning for Bendix Corporation. A UPI release of October 9, 1980, puts it this way:

> Mary E. Cunningham, whose rapid rise in corporate ranks at Bendix Corp. prompted rumors of romantic involvement with Chairman William Agee, resigned today as vice president for strategic planning.
>
> Cunningham, 29, said she resigned because the "widespread publicity given to unfounded rumors" about her relationship with Agee made her position with the auto parts manufacturer "no longer practicable."
>
> Agee, who staunchly defended Cunningham's recent appointment to a vice presidency in the giant corporation, issued a personal statement on her resignation:
>
> "Mary's departure from Bendix is, and will be, an important loss to the company," he said. "She has made an outstanding contribution during her tenure and her exceptional intelligence, intellectual honesty and integrity will be sorely missed.
>
> "The maturity, courage, and professionalism with which she has addressed and resolved this difficult situation are testimony to her unique abilities."
>
> Cunningham, a graduate of the Harvard Business School, said her resignation is effective today. She did not say what her plans were for the immediate future.[4]

This article, as well as others that I saw, was accompanied by a picture of Mary Cunningham, a very attractive woman.

I believe this incident received national attention for two reasons. One reason is that it brought to the surface a universal raw fear in men. Most basically, the fear is: "I'm not going to make it." Fleshed out, the fear looks like this: "I'm having trouble enough trying to make it without more competition. If part of the new competition includes women who are both well trained and aggressive on one hand, and very attractive on the other, then I'm in trouble. Such a woman can alternate the tools for advancement—using her skills one time, and her feminine charm the next time. Against such competition I don't have a chance."

This fear is closely related to the second reason that the Mary Cunningham incident created such interest. The second reason is this: We lack ground rules for fair competition between men and women pursuing the same work rewards. Men know quite well how to compete with other men for promotions, recognition, raises in pay. Lacking the same sort of ground rules for competition between men and women, we have instead a set of suspicions about our opposite-sex competitors. It may look something like this:

A man thinks: She is sleeping her way to the top.

A woman thinks: He is using the exclusive male domains, such as the bar, the club, the locker room to build unfair alliances and push his advantage.

A man thinks: She is using the laws about non-discrimination against women to advance faster than she deserves.

A woman thinks: He is using all those years of corporate experience to find ways to get around the laws, and thus to deny my rights as a worker.

And on and on. As long as this aura of suspicion prevails, a fair system of competition is not likely to emerge.

How do we find our way out of this impasse? We might begin by revising our view of competition itself. Some competition seems to be implicit in the nature of things. More people want to be leaders than there are leadership positions available. But we have fallen into a pattern in which competition becomes an end in itself. The need to "win," to succeed at everything, and sometimes to put the other competitor down, can only be unhealthy. Such an attitude carries anger and hurt for the "loser." Each of us should repeat the following each day: "I'd like to be promoted, but if I lose the competition, it's not the end of the world."

We might continue by recognizing our worth as workers, whether the work we do carries prestige or not. Some people are much better workers than managers; better scientists than administrators of departments; better teachers than principals. If one does well, does one *have* to advance? (And what is advancement?) Isn't it possible that the satisfaction of a job well done is "advancement?"

And we need to discuss openly where the decisions about job rewards are made. How can these processes be made visible, above board, equally accessible to all? That goal will probably never be perfectly realized. Still, an atmosphere of open and fair availability for all is a worthy objective for all of us who work.

Men and Women as Work Colleagues

Dealing with each other as colleagues is closely related to the competition issues we were just mentioning, for today's colleague may be tomorrow's competitor. Quite apart from that, other questions of how to establish a good atmosphere in which one can work compatibly with other persons are also important.

We men find ourselves being expected to change a number of attitudes and actions. We are asked to change our vocabulary. We are not to use the term "ladies" (that belongs in an age of chivalry, not partnership) or the term "girls" (that has a paternalistic, overbearing feel about it) and certainly not the term "my girl" (the puzzled male executive may use the term "my girl" unthinkingly as shorthand for "the highly skilled employee who helps manage responsibilities," but to the employee this term smacks of ownership and slavery).

We are asked to change subtle attitudes. We should not expect that at a committee meeting it will always be one of the women who takes the notes. We are asked not to expect that it will automatically be one of the women who serves the coffee, or who clears away things after a working luncheon.

One woman executive expressed it this way:

> My boss and I have a pretty good relationship, but not as good as he thinks. He thinks he knows how to work with women. He gives me a hug each day, and often tells me how nice I look. That's OK, I like to be told I look nice, but less often would be fine. I'd rather he'd talk to me about my contribution to the work we are doing. What does he think of my effort? Am I making a creative contribution? How can I improve?
>
> I remember one day at a board meeting when I was going to make a really important presentation. I was passing out the outline. I was really nervous about how I was going to do, and one of my co-workers took me by the arm and said "How lovely you are, today." He thought that was a nice compliment, but it didn't feel like one at that moment. I was making the most important presentation of my career, and he was reducing me to being a pretty face.

Her experience reminds us of the comment that in our society too often a woman is first and foremost a body, a body with a mind, but most basically a body. A man is able to be first and foremost a mind, a mind that has a body. If we carry that sort of thinking to our relationships at work, it can interfere with building constructive working relationships.

Barbara Benedict Bunker and Edith Whitfield Seashore point out the non-win situation for the woman if men relate to women in the workplace on the basis of attractiveness:

If the man does not find the woman physically appealing, he may discount her and not give her a chance to be accepted for her competence.

If the man does find the woman physically appealing he may either
—interact with her seductively, testing her to see how she will respond, or
—withdraw from her, because he cannot deal with his own sexual feelings, when he is around her.

In any of these situations, the woman worker loses![5]

Closely related to the issue of physical attractiveness is the theme most frequently mentioned in man-woman work relationships, sexual harassment. A recent survey of a group of workers showed that even after omitting the minor harassments, 30 percent of the women and 9 percent of the men felt they had been sexually harassed at work. The term "sexual harassment" is used more broadly than one might think and includes inappropriate language, sexual innuendos in conversation, touching, patting, fondling, and making sexual demands with implied promises or threats about work connected to the demands.

Some of the men and women with whom I conversed felt that the sexual harassment issue is overstated on two grounds. For one thing, they point out that some persons give out many nonverbal sexual invitations— dress, walk, looks, etc.—and then express outrage when someone responds verbally. Further, some say that sexual comments have just been a normal part of the good-humored kidding around the office.

Be that as it may, unwanted statements or actions are part of a troubled atmosphere at work. Some read this harassment as a statement of anger or hostility at women who have invaded a "man's" domain. Others see it as a male's inappropriate, one-track approach to the females with whom he works. All this suggests that we men need to move to a better level of awareness of women as fellow workers, as persons, and as friends.

This is not to deny that warmth between people—warmth that has sexual overtones—may often develop at work. After all, close association day in and day out, sharing struggles, joys, failures, triumphs is a bonding experience.

But if I respond to people as people, whatever sex they may be; if I am open to them; if I give each person a chance to prove his or her worth on the work team; if I am willing to live with the flow; then perhaps I can be a part of building a better work atmosphere for all, including me.

"All of this is interesting," you say, "but how do I work day in and day out with women colleagues?" These are several things you can do:

(a) Come to terms with your own sexual hangups. If you evaluate all women, including colleagues, on the basis of romance or sex, you need to discover some other ways of relating. If you think that because women menstruate, they are more moody or emotional than you, you have little understanding of your own moods and feelings.

(b) Apply a little of your wisdom in working with male colleagues to working with female ones. When a new male comes on the job, he is accepted on the basis of whether he can do the job, whether he can learn to fit into your working group, and whether he can learn your ways of working together. Treat a woman colleague the same way.

(c) If there are situations in which you are uncertain about how to relate to a woman, ask her. Would she like to be included if the whole work group goes out for lunch together or socializes for an hour after work? Ask her.

(d) Be sensitive to the fact that romantic rumors can be detrimental to both of your marriages (if either of you is married) and both of your careers. Her career will probably be hurt more than yours. Be considerate and remember your prime reason for being at work. A simple summary of advice is: treat your women colleagues as persons.

Men Learning to Work with Women Bosses

"Do you know anyone who is working for a woman boss?" I sometimes ask my male friends. "Yes, me," responded Pete, who works in the computer department of a medium-sized corporation. "What's it like?" I asked. "Nothing unusual," he answered. "She is brand-new, and so it's about like working for any greenhorn boss. We'll give her about the same amount of time to learn the ropes of running the department before we decide how we feel about her as a boss." I commented how down-to-earth and matter-of-factly he was reacting to this rather new phenomenon at work, and he responded, "My mother exerted strong leadership in our family. I have sung under a number of woman choir directors. I have taken several courses from woman professors." "But," I objected, "those are all much more traditional roles for women." "Maybe so," he answered, "but those experiences taught me to respond first to a person's competence and leadership skills. These can be good, bad, or average in either sex!"

We could all learn a lesson from Pete. He not only models how to go to work for a woman boss, but he also suggests that maybe we make the changing work scene a more complicated problem than it needs to be. We simply need to respond to the people we work with as people. How simple it sounds and how difficult it seems to be put into operation.

Out of his experience in counseling many men in the workplace, James Kilgore urges men who work for women to get in touch with their basic fear of change. After they have done that, they are to do the following:

> First, see this woman in your life as you would a man. Yes, that's right! I am assuming that you might see him on the basis of his performance, not his clothing, his emotions, or the color of his hair. You might even try to find some way to identify with him! Give her that chance, too.
> Second, see her abilities and performance before you see her sexuality. Look at how she functions as a supervisor, as an administrator, or a negotiator. Look at what she does and not at what she is. An amazing change might take place—you might like who she is in spite of yourself!

Finally, I borrow a word from the greatest of teachers: treat her as you would like to be treated. He said, "Do unto others as you would have them do to you." And he didn't exclude women from that statement.[6]

As we all respond openly to these changes in the workplace, it is possible that all of us will benefit. In principle we believe in equal opportunity for all. Our workplace gives us an opportunity to put our principles into action.

11

The Tender Mercies
of the God Who Bore Us

Reconsidering Theology, Bible, and Worship

As change comes upon us, one thing we men hate to do is give up an area of life where we either had sole control or predominance. One such area is organized religion. In the past, ordained clergy and the most powerful lay persons have been almost exclusively male. We prayed to a male God. Although women were present in large number— indeed they often worshiped and served more faithfully than we privileged males—they did the more menial tasks. Their behind-the-scenes work frequently made it possible for men to have leadership with very little effort. But now all of that is crumbling, explosively.

Now we need to consider a rather thorny subject: the present state of organized religion and the feminist critique of it. This is a difficult, often divisive topic that I would rather avoid. And yet, I cannot avoid it, for so many people I care about are hurting on both sides of this issue.

I consider the viewpoints about male/female roles in religion to lie along a scale from 1 to 10.

The point of view at number 1 on this scale goes something like this:

The religious institution is basically as it should be if the protesters would just go away. As C. S. Lewis once wrote, "God Himself has taught us how to speak of Him. To say that it does not matter is to say either that all the masculine imagery is not inspired, is merely human in origin, or else that, though inspired, it is quite arbitrary and unessential." [1] The male references to God are necessary and integral.

Furthermore, God created the priesthood and entrusted it to men.

115

This has been true for centuries; see where the court of women was in the temple in Jerusalem. This is not a put-down of women. It simply describes a difference of function. As God has entrusted motherhood to women, so has God entrusted the priesthood, and certainly the administering of baptism and the Lord's Supper, to men. Scripture teaches this, and there is nothing anyone can do about it but accept it; that's the way it is.

The advocate of this position hopes that women will understand its logic and reasonableness and find their place within it.

At the extreme opposite end of this scale, at number 10, the viewpoint would be something like this:

If God is male, then the male is God, and that is the way it seems to be in Christianity. The Bible was written by men, for men, assuming male leadership in service of a male God. The myths, images, symbols, language of this religion are male through and through. They use such terms as Father, patriarch, king, lord, Saviour, Messiah, and even God. Why not Goddess?

The structure of the church is patriarchal and hierarchical—one male commanding and dominating another. The most dominated male at least has women beneath him.

This stern, paternalistic, warrior, male God has inspired the most atrocious wars. Persons still seem to be able to pray to this God and ignore the oppression of most of the world. There is no place for a woman in such a church or religion. A new language of the transcendent, a new understanding of what it means to be in harmony with the divine one, a new community, a new way of relating is what we need.

The proponent of this position will regretfully write Christianity off as archaic and irrelevant. That person will attempt to discover or create a religious system without the encumbrances that alienate him or her from this one.

Viewpoint number 5 on this scale understands what both 1 and 10 are saying and feels the tug of each. But number 5 feels that both 1 and 10 have missed or ignored some important considerations. The number 5 position is something like this:

While it is true there is much male language in the Bible, that is not its most basic essence. The central theme of the Bible is a God who acts to redeem and liberate people, a God who loves and frees people, a God who helps them become new persons, a God who helps them claim and develop marvelous gifts. This God empowers people with the Spirit, calls them into a loving community, and sends them forth into the world as agents of divine compassion and reconciliation.

This community, the church, that God calls forth has been renewed, reformed, revived, changed, led in new directions many times in church history. Believers sense that these new directions are guided by God's creative Spirit. One church leader once told us that in history there is still more light and truth to break forth out of God's Holy Word. Rather than give up on the church, persons might view the unrest in the church today as the first signs of another possible reformation.

Persons holding this position are sometimes strengthened by their church family and sometimes frustrated by it; but they continue their "lover's quarrel" with it, in the hope that it can become more responsive to their concerns.

Individuals who hold positions 1, 5, and 10 are good people. They may be lovers of God and committed to Christ and church. They may even enjoy each other and work side by side. But when this issue surfaces, they feel a sharp division.

It appears to me that the issues involving the changing male, feminism, and the church come down to five basic questions: (1) How shall we speak of God? (2) How shall we translate and interpret the Bible? (3) What shall be our language and style of worship? (4) Shall we recognize, affirm, and use the gifts of all? and (5) In the light of all this, does the nature and purpose of the church need to be reexamined?

Let me frankly say at the outset that I am going to attempt to deal with these questions from a 5 position, while at the same time trying to be sensitive to positions 1 and 10. I write as one who is greatly enriched by the Christian faith community and am saddened when any feel that they must leave that community because it has not heard their cry. I write as one who has not been as hurt on some of these issues as some of my sisters in the faith, but who has much to learn from the discoveries gained in this struggle. So let's explore these issues.

How Shall We Speak of God?

Most frequently we speak of God by using metaphors, terms from human experience that tell us in some small way what God is like.

The Bible frequently uses metaphors to speak about God. The Bible also contains a firm prohibition against idolatry, substituting anything for God as the object of worship. And so to take any one metaphor about God and absolutize it, make it *the* description of God, is idolatry.[2] Perhaps we have fallen into a subtle idolatry by absolutizing one metaphor about God, God the Father.

Bible writers use masculine, feminine, and neuter metaphors about God. Some of the neuter metaphors suggest God is like a wall, shield, fortress, rock, sword, word, glory, morning dew, light, etc. These metaphors may spark a moment of insight, may cause a person to take time to pause and reflect a moment. But they stir no great excitement, emotion, or identification.

It is the masculine and feminine metaphors about God that stir our identifying emotions and fill us with either excitement or revulsion. Let us look first at the female metaphors for God that are used in the Bible.

The Bible portrays God as *mother;* God gives birth.

> You were unmindful of the Rock that begot you,
>   and you forgot the God who gave you birth.
>   —Deuteronomy 32:18 (see also Isaiah 42:14)

God also provides the traditional motherly nurturing.

> When Israel was a child, I loved him,
>   and out of Egypt I called my son. . . .
> It was I who taught Ephraim to walk,
>   I took them up in my arms:
>   but they did not know that I healed them.
>   —Hosea 11:1,3

> As one whom his mother comforts,
>   so I will comfort you;
>   —Isaiah 66:13*a*

> "Can a woman forget her suckling child,
>   that she should have no compassion on the son of
>   her womb?"
> Even these may forget,
>   yet I will not forget you.
>   —Isaiah 49:15

The Bible portrays God as *midwife* and *nursemaid*. In a passage that mixes male and female imagery, God is perceived as saying:

> "Hearken to me, O house of Jacob,
>   all the remnant of the house of Israel,
> who have been borne by me from your birth,
>   carried from the womb;
> even to your old age I am He,
>   and to gray hairs I will carry you.
> I have made, and I will bear;
>   I will carry and will save.
>   —Isaiah 46:3-4

Other passages that portray God as midwife include Psalm 22:9 and Isaiah 66:9.

God is portrayed as performing culturally assigned "womanly" tasks of providing food for the children in Israel in the wilderness (Exodus 16) and of clothing both Adam and Eve and the children of Israel (Genesis 3:21).

Jesus compares God to a housekeeper, scouring her house until she finds the coin she has lost (Luke 15:8-10). At the time this was a radical image. As Virginia Ramey Mollenkott has pointed out, "In order to feel the full impact of this image of God as a woman, we must remind ourselves of the patriarchal culture of rabbinic Judaism which tolerated the concept that a man's wickedness is better than a woman's goodness."[3]

Further, there are images, terms in the Bible that the Hebews would recognize as female metaphors or images of God that we do not.

For example, the word for womb or uterus in Hebrew is *rehem*. The plural of *rehem* is *rahamim* which usually means not "wombs" but rather "the abstract qualities of compassion, mercy and love." In the Bible, then, compassion is "womb-love," or mother love, or the love of a woman for the one whom she has borne. In Jeremiah 31:20 God says,

> Is Ephraim my dear son?
> Is he my darling child?
> For as often as I speak against him,
> I do remember him still,
> Therefore my heart yearns for him;
> I will surely have mercy on him, says the Lord.

In this passage the term "mercy" in the last line is literally motherly compassion, or "womb-love."[4] (See also Psalm 71:6; Isaiah 49:1.)

Another Hebrew concept that was decidedly feminine was *hokmah* a term translated "wisdom." Wisdom was personified as a woman, and she offered God's guidance to all who would listen. Wisdom danced before God and was the enabling power at creation (see all of Proverbs 8, but especially verses 22-36). First Corinthians 1:24 and 30 make clear to us that this female image, wisdom, is applied to Jesus, for Jesus is described as the "wisdom of God."

Other Bible terms that were considered female by the Hebrews were: *Torah*—law, teaching, instruction; *shekinah*—the glory of God, which is God's presence as manifest on earth; and *ruach*—spirit or wind. Spirit is considered feminine in the Hebrew, the language of the Old Testament. Spirit is considered neuter in Greek, the language of the

New Testament. Jesus alludes to the Hebrew concept of spirit as feminine in John 3:5, when he says one must be born of water and the spirit. The Spirit of God gives birth to us in the second birth.

The fact that these female metaphors about God were used in a culture in which women had rather low status makes their impact all the stronger. These biblical passages stretch our thinking and the ways we can speak of God.

Now let us look at male metaphors for God in the Bible. Metaphors ascribed to God came from both political and pastoral life. These terms included: "king," "judge," "lord," and "shepherd."

Some of the male metaphors for God came from family life, such as: "redeemer," "brother," "kinsman," and "father." The intent in using the metaphor "father" for God was to emphasize that God is a "gracious, caring, faithful, wise, ethically sensitive, and unsurpassed sovereign."[5] In Romans 8:15-16 we read, "When we cry 'Abba! Father!' it is the Spirit himself bearing witness with our spirit that we are children of God. . . ." I am told that the term there, "Abba," can be properly translated "Papa," or "Daddy," a term of family love and closeness.

Unfortunately, the image of "Father God" has often been misinterpreted. People take it to mean a judgmental, patriarchal tyrant. Shusaku Endo, Catholic Japanese novelist, has attempted a subtle reinterpretation of Christianity to make it more understandable and acceptable in Japan. Endo feels that what must be given up is Western Christianity's emphasis on the fatherhood of God "with its overtones of patriarchal omnipotence and judgment."[6] Endo quotes an old Japanese proverb which says that the four most awful things on earth are "fires, earthquakes, thunderbolts, and fathers." In his touching book, *A Life of Jesus,* Endo portrays Jesus as a sensitive, loving person, who in the crucifixion is seen as feeble and helpless; his death is that of any powerless, ineffectual man. Endo points out that Jesus was put to death by a people he never ceased to love. His resurrection was his response to their betrayal with love. In so doing Jesus revealed the "maternal aspect of God."[7] As *Newsweek* puts it, "He (Endo) urges a 'motherhood' of God which he feels is truer both to the New Testament and to Japanese experience. The Japanese venerate their mothers, and, in religion, the maternal image. Christianity, Endo concludes, will thrive in Japan only when the church appropriates this feeling to its traditional Son of God."[8]

At any rate, the male metaphors of God have prevailed and are in wide use while the female ones are barely noted. Jesus, the promised one, was born a male. It could hardly have been otherwise in that culture. Mollenkott points out, however, that when the New Testament writers speak of the incarnation of Jesus they speak of his becoming *anthropos*, human being, rather than becoming *aner*, male. (See, for example, Romans 15:12-15). The important truth of the incarnation is that God came to us in *human* flesh, not male flesh.

The masculine metaphors for God are as helpful as the feminine ones and the neuter ones. However, they should not be absolutized. Krister Stendahl, former dean of Harvard Divinity School points out, "The masculinity of God and of God language is a cultural and linguistic accident, and I think one should argue that the masculinity of the Christ is of the same order." [9]

Perhaps this discussion can enable us to ponder the richness of thought and imagery available in regard to our God. And perhaps it can help us let go of the habit of using just one metaphor for God.

I therefore propose we answer our first question, "How shall we speak of God?" by saying, "With all the diversity of imagery that the Bible uses, but with an adjusted frequency of terms, given the needs of our age."

How Shall We Translate and Interpret the Bible?

Our understanding of the ways we speak of God should help us deal with our next question: What about the Bible? How should we translate it? Interpret it?

In recent times there have been newspaper articles that claim that the RSV Bible committee is going to "unman" or "neuter" or "de-sex" the Bible. These claims are exaggerated and untrue. Two things are happening in regard to the Bible of which we should be aware.

First, the Revised Standard Version Bible committee is working on a revision of this most widely used Bible. The members of this committee have agreed to listen to suggestions about inclusive language in the Bible but will follow these suggestions only when they coincide with the original Hebrew, Greek, or Aramaic words.

There are places in the Bible which show the effect of translators who lived in male-dominated cultures. These translators used masculine nouns and pronouns not found in the original texts, and these can be properly changed. There are Hebrew or Greek terms which can be more generally translated "human" than "man," and this can be done and still be faithful to the Bible text.

Second, the Education and Ministry Committee of the National Council of Churches voted to produce an inclusive language translation of the lectionary. (The lectionary is a collection of Scripture used by many churches for worship on a calendarized basis.) This will be a paraphrase of these selected Scripture passages along the lines we indicated in the previous section. It will use language that does not exclude women or make them appear secondary in the eyes of God or the church. Inclusive language will be included in the words used about God. While work has not yet begun on this new lectionary, Blaine Fister suggests that some of the changes will look like this:

a) Words like "men" and "sons" will be changed to "men and women" or "human beings" and "sons and daughters" or "children."
b) Words referring to God will include both masculine and feminine images. The words used will also describe the God we know, not as a human being but as our creator, redeemer, and comforter. The pronoun "He" will be avoided simply by avoiding the use of pronouns to describe God.[10]

What should we make of these efforts? I am personally quite comfortable with the first of the two efforts that I described: the revision of the RSV Bible with careful attention to the original text. That careful dialogue between the original text and today's issues can be eagerly anticipated.

The revision of the lectionary is a much more sweeping effort. This will be a paraphrase, not a translation of the Bible. As long as we know what we are reading, paraphrases can be quite useful. J. B. Phillips' *The Bible in Today's English* and *The Living Bible* are both paraphrases, enjoyed by many for the vivid, contemporary feeling they convey. A paraphrase that communicates the Spirit of God's inclusiveness, even when the words do not, is appropriate so long as we also keep in touch with Bible versions that more accurately communicate the original text.

What Shall Be Our Language and Style of Worship?

Don Postema shares a fantasy about visiting a church:

When he entered the church, he was seated by a woman usher. A quick glance at the bulletin revealed an all-woman council. Then at 10:00 A.M. a woman entered the pulpit to lead the service.

The minister gave the Call to Worship:

"Our help is in the name of the Creator who made heaven and earth. When anyone is united with Christ, she is a new person. Welcome to this service in the Name of God, the Creator, the Redeemer, and the Sanctifier; the God of Sarah, Rebekah, and Rachel, of Deborah, Lydia and Priscilla. So be it."

He felt excluded from the service from the start. He felt even more excluded when the clergy woman asked them to greet each other, "Since you have all been greeted by God, and since you are all sisters in Christ, you can now greet others of the sisterhood."

When he visited with others, he was asked, "Are you single?" "And what does your wife do? Is she here on business? How many children do you have?''

Then he read the New Testament lesson from 1 John 2:9-10. ''She who says she is in the light and hates her sister is in the darkness still. She who loves her sister abides in the light. . . .'' He felt very uncomfortable.

''The sermon . . . was addressed to sisters and to the feminine experiences in society. The minister didn't even try to speak to me or the other men in the congregation. She gave the impression that to be a person was to be a sister! It was like eavesdropping on a conversation for women only.

''Do I belong here? Prayers, creeds, hymns, even sermon—always feminine when referring to people. But I am not and never will be a female, a sister. Do I belong? Am I invisible? They greeted me but then seemed to forget I was there. Do I really matter to them? to God? Does God like me as I am—male? She urged them to be 'new women.' What about me? How can I be a new woman?''[11]

Postema's fantasy may make us men aware of what we unthinkingly do to women in Christian worship. Perhaps this realization makes us ready to hear these hopes about language in worship from Ann Patrick Ware.

> The language of worship must change to include women. Away with such terms as ''brethren,'' ''fraternal,'' ''every man,'' ''mankind,'' and a host of others. Down with hymns like ''Once to Every Man and Nation,'' ''Rise Up, O Men of God,'' ''Good Christian Men, Rejoice,'' ''Faith of our Fathers,'' etc. The language of worship must change so as not to subordinate or ridicule women. No more references to the church as ''she,'' to God as ''he.'' No more mother-in-law jokes, ''little old ladies in tennis shoes,'' or ''old wives' tales'' in the sermon. The biblical passages read for worship must be cleaned up of their sexist words and innuendos, for the church cannot afford to have a sacred book which fosters discrimination. The preaching style must change from that of superior enlightenment to one of comradely exploration. If we are to be equals, an exquisite sensitivity to the ''other'' must be resplendent in all we say and do. The place to start is by having our language reflect that sensitivity.[12]

Such an enthusiastic ringing call sounds good until I stop to reflect. I plan, design, and lead many worship services. The issue I constantly live with in planning worship is this: how do I plan appropriate words and actions and rituals for the extremely varied community that will worship together? That is never easy, and even more difficult if we take into consideration the issue Ann Patrick Ware raises with us.

When I lead a worship service, I can sense when people are struggling and when they are participating wholeheartedly. And I can be sure that when we pray the Lord's Prayer (Our father. . . .'') and sing the doxology (". . . Praise Father, Son, and Holy Ghost'') participation becomes solid and assured. Christian feminist friends tell me, however, that they are suffering pain at that very moment. I'm sure that things are happening on several different levels when we pray that prayer and sing that song. For one thing, we are creatures of habit. We have come to expect those moments in worship. Further, they are familiar and traditional. We sense that we join with generations before us and (perhaps) after us who make the same affirmations. Rightly or wrongly, we often look to worship as something predictable and stable in a world quaking with change.

Linda J. Clark speaks of this issue as she discusses "consensus."

Worship is an act of the gathered church and is, therefore, public and communal. Its language must have some vital connection to the life of the people who use it. In any group there exists an unspoken consensus about the meaning of the words it uses. Changes in that consensus take time. Women contend that the language of liturgy excludes them and does not express their perception of God; yet the changes they propose do not reflect a consensus of the feelings within the Christian community. There has to be a period of "speechlessness"—a period of give-and-take during which the community of the church learns to expand the consensus of meaning to include the new insights contributed by women about the nature of God and the human community. This process of change is gradual and emotion-laden.[13]

How then do we worship in this interim period, this time of change, this period of "speechlessness"? Several considerations occur to me.

It won't be possible to eliminate all unintentional sexist language of the centuries at once in most "churches that are." Small intentional congregations founded by people who are willing to experiment may well be able to do so from the outset.

In the meantime, there are many steps that can be taken. The biblical references cited above in the discussion of the language about God can be amply used in worship. Worship leaders and preachers can take care to use inclusive language and can ask for help in recognizing when they slip away from it. Small, innovative worship services—say with youth groups, or with adult groups in camp and retreat settings—can introduce the totally inclusive language of worship. For the most part these will be efforts of addition rather than subtraction.

We can create new hymns, prayers, liturgy, literature. Recently I read a powerful and helpful book by a wife and husband team (*The Transforming Cross* by Charles S. McCoy and Marjorie C. McCoy [Nashville: Abingdon Press, 1978]). I was two-thirds of the way through before it even occurred to me that here was a Christian devotional book, probing the meaning of the cross, written in inclusive language. These authors made me aware of an excellent strategy, bring in the new with enthusiasm, creativity, and joy. If we can do so, our vision will gradually be incorporated into the lives of those we influence.

Although we cannot bring about the sudden changes some would prefer, our goal must be total inclusiveness. After noting reasons for the difficulty and change of language, Linda J. Clark notes the benefits that come from persisting on this course.

> Shifting the language of worship to sex-inclusive language rather than sex-exclusive—either male or female—works against the oppression of women and helps to build up the community of faith. The use of metaphors and other expressions that affirm that women, too, were created in the image of God will help to accomplish this. Our language about God will expand to include those traits normally associated with women. It will bring to consciousness the experiences of God that deepen and enrich our faith. It will gradually eliminate the oppression of women in the Christian community. Through the explicit association of female images with God, the source of ultimate value, the female person will have greater value, the implication being that women, too, have godlike qualities.[14]

Ann Patrick Ware concludes the essay quoted earlier by saying, "The Sunday shepherds preach their Good News for Modern Man but it falls on feminist ears as Bad News for Us Ewes. Dear brothers, if you want to keep us in your midst, wise up, O men of God!"[15]

12

The Tender Mercies (Continued)

Adjusting to the Changing Church

L et's ask two more questions that continue the quest we began last chapter.

Shall We Recognize and Use the Gifts of All?

To translate this question into more direct terms: Are we going to accept women as church leaders, whether the leadership be voluntary or paid, lay or professional, educational or pastoral, ordained or not? Are we men going to use our gifts in the church disregarding the usual sex stereotypes?

There is probably no area of church life in which the leadership and participation is closed to us males if we choose to participate. The question we need to face is this: Are we going to open up all areas of the life of the church to all—males and females alike? Are we going to claim the gifts of all? If our sisters and daughters sense that they have heard the call to ordained ministry, will they be allowed to be ordained? Will they be extended a call to serve a church as pastor?

For a long time, the answer to this question has been no. Some major branches of the Christian church still do not ordain women. Only 4 percent of all the clergy in those denominations which do ordain are women. And only 2.2 percent of the total clergy in the country are women.

My denomination is one that has granted ordination to women for nearly a century. And yet a recent, careful sociological study revealed that the acceptance of women in ministry is much less than complete. When the study compared the experience of three years' classes of women seminary graduates with a comparable number of men seminary graduates, they found the following:

> There is evidence of discrimination in the seminaries, among executive and area ministers [those who work directly with churches in selecting pastors in my democratic polity denomination], among pulpit committee representatives, and among the laity in general. The women candidates perceive themselves being less accepted as ministers than men. Furthermore, the number of contacts they have, the salary and allowances they enjoy and the amount of time it takes for them to be placed indicates that the problem is not just with the women's perceptions but indeed does reside in virtually all segments of the recruitment/placement system itself.[1]

But, many persons may ask, doesn't the Bible clearly say that women should not be in ministry? First Corinthians 14:33b and the verses following tell us,

As in all the churches of the saints, the women should keep silence in the churches. For they are not permitted to speak, but should be subordinate, as even the law says. If there is anything they desire to know, let them ask their husbands at home. For it is shameful for a woman to speak in church.

First Timothy 2:11-12 adds, "Let a woman learn in silence with all submissiveness. I permit no woman to teach or to have authority over men; she is to keep silent."

What about such biblical passages? There are several observations to be made about these and other New Testament passages on the subject. First, we need to realize that these passages dealt with the subject of order in public worship. The problem in Corinth was disorderly worship; everyone wanted to talk, to participate in a wild, enthusiastic worship. Paul is advising the church how to keep some order in that situation. The word "speak" is used twenty-four times in 1 Corinthians 14. Everyone wanted to "speak," but the term does not mean formal lecture, sermon, or teaching. It means simply talking, even idle talk or chatter.[2] And so 1 Corinthians 14 is a comment about a local worship problem; it is not a once and for all statement about whether women belong in pulpits or not.

Hardesty and Scanzoni point out that the 1 Timothy 2:11-12 passage probably speaks to two concerns: (a) that women without the gift of teaching were usurping this task (and false teaching is one of the great concerns of the first letter to Timothy); (b) that when it says women should not "have authority over men," the word translated "have authority" probably means "dominate or domineer over" and refers to their husbands. Rather than saying no women are qualified for church leadership, it speaks against false teachers and women who may be disrupting their families and marriages.[3]

Both of these passages, then, quite probably deal with local problems and should not be taken as a final statement on women in ministry.

Most Bible scholars agree that the key doctrinal statement Paul makes on this issue is Galatians 3:28, "There is neither Jew nor Greek, there is neither slave nor free, there is neither male nor female [It literally says "There is not male and female"] for you are all one in Christ Jesus." Some Bible scholars feel that Galatians 3:28 is a baptismal formula. Paul quotes it at this key point in the letter because it would come from an even wider authority than his own. "In the new Spirit-filled community of equals all distinctions of race, religion, class, and gender are abolished. . . . By reciting this baptismal formula, the newly initiated Christians expressed their Christian self-understanding."[4]

The New Testament offers ample evidence that women claimed this great affirmation and were a vital part of the early church both as participants and leaders in a wide variety of ways. All four Gospels mention that women were among the followers of Jesus and that they were "the most courageous of all his disciples." (See Mark 15:40-41 particularly).[5] Women leaders present throughout the early church included Christian women prophets (1 Corinthians 11:5). Philip's four daughters (Acts 21:9) are mentioned particularly as prophets.

In Romans 16, Paul greeted twenty-nine people. Of these, ten were women. Included in this list was Phoebe who was given two titles: *(a) diakonos,* (deacon, not deaconess since there is no such term as "deaconess" in Greek) which is usually translated "minister"; *(b) prostatis,* which usually means "president, ruler, superintendent."[6] Quite clearly, Phoebe was a ministerial leader in Rome. In verse 7 of Romans 16, Paul greeted Andronicus and Junia. These two people, man and woman, were given the title of "apostle." Did you get that? The Bible speaks of a woman apostle! This was generally a term reserved for people who had witnessed the resurrection of the Lord and who were commissioned by the resurrected Lord to missionary effort.[7] Paul also spoke about Mary, Tryphaena, Tryphosa, and Persis who "labored hard in the Lord."

Many other women are mentioned in various roles in the early church. Women were among the early, prominent, wealthy converts who influenced the mission of the young church (Acts 17:4, 12). Nympha of Laodicea is mentioned because of the "church in her house" (Colossians 4:15). Acts 18:24-28 tells about Prisca (also known as Priscilla) and her husband, Aquila, who took an active teaching role as they "expounded the way of God more accurately" to a learned Jew from Alexandria. This missionary couple are also remembered for the church in their house (1 Corinthians 16:19; Romans 16:3). The household of a woman named Chloe was also influential in the Corinthian church and supplied the information that occasioned Paul's writing to the Corinthians (1 Corinthians 1:11).

There is now archeological evidence that the church of the early centuries after Christ also granted places of leadership in the church to women. Professor Dorothy Irvin of the College of St. Catherine points to archeological evidence that women received ordination and exercised ministry alongside men in the earliest days of the Christian Church. She points out Roman inscriptions which refer to women as *archisynogogos* (rulers of a synagogue) and *presbytera* (elders). She also takes note of a fresco from the Roman catacombs in which seven first-century women are celebrating the Eucharist (Lord's Supper). Further, she points out a fourth-century fresco of a woman receiving ordination from a bishop. She is aware also of tombstone inscriptions which refer to "honorabilia femina episcopa," which may be translated "honorable woman bishop."[8]

But back to Paul for a moment. With all we have said, we cannot ignore that at times Paul seemed to advocate a quite secondary position for women in the church. Paul often contradicted himself at this point. The reason he did so was that there was a three-sided war going on in his own reasoning involving: *(a)* his rabbinic training, which taught a subservient place for women; *(b)* the culture in which he spoke (he reflects the culture of his day when he talks about "nature itself" or "the very nature of things" in 1 Corinthians 11:14); and *(c)* the liberating implications of the gospel. As we read his writings on this subject, we can see that sometimes one side wins and sometimes the other.

Mollenkott finds it instructive to watch these three influences do battle in Paul's head as he works through a perplexing question. She suggests that when we read his statements on female subordination, which contradict much of his own behavior and other things he wrote, we see "a basically godly human being in process, struggling with his own socialization," and this in turn should force us to use our own heads in working through conflicting evidence.[9]

Dr. Calvin Roetzel points out that "it would be remarkable indeed if Paul did not reflect some of the prejudice, superstition, and bias of his own time. . . . It seems unfair to denounce him for not anticipating and addressing concerns that have only recently been raised to a high level of consciousness. . . . It is the gospel which Paul preaches rather than his limited application and witness to it that is definitive for our time."[10]

Dr. Mollenkott concludes that "the Bible was not in error to record Paul's thought processes. But *we* are in error to absolutize anything that denies the thrust of the entire Bible toward individual wholeness and harmonious community, toward oneness in Christ.''[11]

Contrary to what many people believe, then, the Bible not only gives permission to use all the gifts of sisters and brothers in the faith, but the Bible also declares our sacred oneness and urges all to use their gifts to build up the body of Christ, the church.

I personally believe that there are two significant reasons why we should obey this and work hard at removing all barriers that keep our sisters from full participation in the ordained ministry. First, we damage and hurt persons when they are not allowed to exercise their full range of gifts. I am haunted by the woman quoted by Scanzoni and Hardesty.

> I heard your call to preach your word, but when I sought advice from my pastor he ridiculed me.
> I applied to a seminary, but they told me women were not permitted to enroll in the master of divinity program.
> I requested ordination from our denomination, but they told me women were not called to the ministry.
> I asked to candidate at a local church, but they said people in the congregation would not accept a woman pastor.
> I applied to a mission board, but they turned me away when they learned my gift was evangelization, not nursing, secretarial work, or teaching children.
> So I just gave up, got married, and had kids like everyone had been telling me to do all along.[12]

One of my woman friends tells me she sensed the call to ministry, but her church discouraged her until she gave it up. She says, ''I was both liberated and duped by the same faith community.'' Understandably, she is rather ambivalent about the church.

How tragic if, in any way, we quench the Spirit and deny the gifts in any child of God!

Second, the church has so much to gain from claiming these gifts that are offered. The church needs a wide range of gifts; it needs sensitivity, creativity, enthusiastic service. Since a large number of our sisters are aspiring to offer these gifts, I believe the church should be ready to receive them.

I speak from personal experience. When I was eleven years old, a woman came to be pastor of my home church, and she is my pastor to this day. Before she arrived, it was generally agreed by the people of my little hometown, a ranch and farm town in western South Dakota, that this was no place for a woman pastor, much less one raised in Cambridge, Massachusetts. But she came, lived down those skepticisms, and won persons over with a direct, personal, caring style of ministry. Her personal interest and counsel helped many a young person to dream dreams, make plans, and achieve his or her maximum potential. She helped me explore my call to ministry; encouraged me and aided me in developing my gifts; provided personal, spiritual, and financial help along the way to ordination; consoled, counseled, and guided me in my early days of ministry. In a significant measure, I am what I am today because the grace of God was mediated to me by a woman pastor named Jeanie Sherman. Her influence affects me in the way I live my ministry in many conscious and unconscious ways. I only wish that many more persons shared my experience of receiving the benefits of ministry of a woman pastor. That experience might well prepare us to open the channels of ministry more freely to women considering and entering ministry today.

As Jeanie Sherman has her unique gifts for ministry, so does each person. When the church creates the climate in which those gifts can be more freely explored and expressed, the church will be the richer for it.

I must add that long before most of our churches call woman pastors, we can begin to escape some of the sex-role stereotypes that have prevailed there.

We can elect women to positions of authority. Why is it that even though women have been a large majority of the faithful, some churches have never had a woman moderator or president—or, at most, one or two in a hundred years?

We can elect women to places of influence, such as the board of trustees or finance. (Not just one, maybe a majority.) We can also invite women to be part of the group that gives leadership in such sacraments as baptism and the Lord's Supper. From the above examination of Scripture it becomes clear that it is sexist tradition, not Scripture, that decrees women prepare the elements of the Lord's Supper and wash the dishes afterwards while the men serve those elements publicly.

We males can take our part in the housecleaning chores at church, in preparing, serving, and cleaning up when there is food served (and not just tokenism at a once-a-year mother-daughter banquet), in child care, and in the teaching of small children.

If we take these steps, we may be ready for our woman pastor.

Does the Nature and Purpose of the Church Need to Be Reexamined?

I well remember a conversation I had with friends of mine who are Roman Catholic nuns just after they had returned from a conference on the ordination of women. For that branch of the church, women's ordination seemed a distant goal, and it seems just as far away at the present.

Even though that hope seemed remote and unlikely to happen within their lifetime, they were thrilled by the conference and the fact that it had even occurred. They told me quietly, "We don't simply want to be ordained in the church that is. We want to be ordained so that the church can change." When I asked them what they wanted to change, they mentioned several things:

—the ordained person not as authority but rather as servant and leader of a ministering community;

—less emphasis on the church as a hierarchical institution and more emphasis on the church as a family of believers;

—less emphasis on sacramental ministry and more on person-to-person, caring ministry;

—less emphasis on the huge gathering and more on the small group, intentional and purposeful, able to be in a home.

I didn't tell them, but what they were describing sounded much like the small, rural church of my boyhood pastored by a woman. Of course, their vision, though it had much in common with that experience, had elements of newness in it as well.

Other feminist Christian friends see other possibilities as the church becomes open to their experience and vision.

Said one, "I find it exciting how women are approaching spirituality. We have many perceptions of it, and we don't try to sort and give one perception a top position. We sense that no one has a corner on truth. Rather, there is room for all of us. Truth contains all of us. We are enriched by one another."

Said another, "From my involvement in the Christian feminist movement I see the coming of more humanized power, greater freedom to celebrate and talk about the spiritual dimension of life, and less repression of the sublime spirituality of one's life. I see more celebration and more support."

Perhaps that "gentle revolution" of which they speak may be the greatest gift that women will bring to the church that is open to receive it. The excitement of being part of the Christian church is that, time and again throughout history, God has renewed and revived the church from unexpected sources. May it be possible that God renew the church through this resource:

A richly varied vision of who God is,

A rethinking of the reign of God in human lives,

A rediscovery of the church's inherent nature,

A group of people empowered by the recognition

of their gifts and the authority of their call.
Do not the seeds of renewal seem to be here?

In that renewed church men and women will celebrate God's lovely and varied grace. Made new by that grace, they will be renewed in the search of discovering "the things that make for peace."

And Finally

While doing my research on this subject, I came upon an article that made me aware of how delicate and urgent it is that we men within the church be sensitive to the issues that women are raising with us. I can quote but a few paragraphs from this article. Please ponder them carefully.

> Women's liberation is a *conversion experience*. For many women (and men) their conversion to the women's movement will be one of the two or three radical changes in their lives. A woman experiences vague apprehensions, an inchoate uneasiness. She feels she is odd because she is not always happy with the roles expected of her in society. She talks with other women, and she finds that they share many of the same feelings. Suddenly it becomes clear. There is nothing wrong with her. The problem is that "women's role" does not fit women. The experience is sweet. "Liberation" is no longer a word; it becomes a deep penetrating sense of her potential.
>
> From this new perspective nothing is left unchallenged. One day a woman realizes that something she has held sacred—her parents' ideal for her life, a favorite story from childhood or adolescence, a dream she has had about life—is part of a vast social mythology which keeps women in the inner space and refuge of home and family.
>
> Conversion to women's liberation is structurally similar to conversion to a new religious consciousness. In this sense, women's liberation itself partakes of the numinous. Like other conversion experiences it is frightening as well as liberating. Social structures and institutions which had defined social reality are experienced as arbitrary and alienating. The center of reality changes[13] (italics added).

Christ and Collins help us see the power, depth, and significance of the women's movement for some women by pointing out to us that women's liberation is a *conversion* experience. When one is converted, one has personally appropriated truth so powerful that life must be reorganized around that truth.

They say further that, structurally, this conversion is similar to conversion to a new religious consciousness. Is it a religious conversion similar to others? (After all, the Bible never says you can only be converted once.) Some persons would answer no; this is a quite secular conversion experience. But others may well intuit that this conversion has Christian and biblical dimensions.

It is a discovery of one's potential and gifts, a Christian concept.

It is awareness of one's worth as a person in the image of God, a Christian concept.

It is being liberated, set free, again a Christian image.

For the woman who sees the divine dimension in this experience, it is important that this dimension be preserved. It is equally important that if a woman senses that her church has spoken to her of her worth, gifts, and liberation and has had a part in this discovery/conversion, she then should also feel the support of the church as she implements the vision. Otherwise, a quite understandable but tragic sense of betrayal and anger will follow.

I trust it is obvious that I write with the hope that men will similarly be set free: free from the bondage of dehumanizing societal and cultural expectations; free from role expectations that isolate us from our own emotions and from those we would like to love; free from the need to compete and prove something; free to commit, to love, to become. If we are indeed free from and for all this, it can then be said of us as well, "Men's liberation is a conversion experience."

13

A New Vision, a New Freedom

The Liberated Man from the Christian Perspective

It is a fact that more women are involved in liberation issues than men. It is also a fact that these women approach these subjects with more commitment, urgency and zeal than men. The reason for this difference seems to be both that women experience more dissatisfaction with the present state of things and that they see more potential gain for themselves beyond the present pain.

As one man who elected to be part of a men's awareness group I was leading told me, "I need to talk about these issues, but all I see is more loss. I don't see much payoff for me."

Well, I disagree.

What men will lose in the liberation movement is minor compared to what they may gain. The possible gain for men comes in greater possibilities, a wider range of choices, a less lonely world, the potential of being more helpful to others, and much more.

Charlotte Clinebell notes that many persons who are struggling with these liberation issues come for counseling with two questions: "How do I become a whole person?" and "What *is* a whole person?"[1] To face these questions head on is, in itself, a liberating experience.

In response, Clinebell points to the new-old term that some psychologists are now using, the term *androgyny*. This term comes from the two Greek words *andros* (which means "male") and *gyne* (which means "female"). The androgynous person is the one who can be a whole person by expressing, experiencing, and acting in the ways that culture has usually associated with being male *and* with being female.

Sandra Bem, a psychologist who has done much work in this field, describes the androgynous person as one who is able to be either instrumental *or* expressive, assertive *or* yielding, independent *or* playful—in other words to behave appropriately as the situation requires."[2]

Bem notes of course that however psychologically androgynous we become, we are still physically male or female. We will have a male or female body build, female or male genitalia, the capability of either becoming pregnant or impregnating. And she says that to be psychologically healthy one must have a healthy sense of one's physical maleness or physical femaleness. She continues, "But I would argue that a healthy sense of maleness or femaleness involves little more than being able to look into the mirror and to be perfectly comfortable with the body that one sees there."[3] That is to say, that one's physical maleness or femaleness is not one's entire destiny. Just because one can become pregnant does not mean that she should do so, or that she should accept domestic homemaking and child care as her prime role. Just because a male can impregnate does not mean he should do so, nor does it mean that he should be excluded from domestic homemaking or child care, simply because of his physical maleness.

Masculinity and femininity each have a tendency to become negative and perhaps even destructive when they are present in extreme form without the presence of the opposite. "Extreme femininity, untempered by a sufficient concern for one's own needs as an individual, may produce dependency and self-denial, just as extreme masculinity, untempered by a sufficient concern for the needs of others, may produce arrogance and exploitation."[4]

She points out that the basic task of every organism is somehow to find balance between "agency (productiveness)" and "communion (relatedness)." Thus, if masculinity and femininity are tempered into the other and integrated into a balanced, more fully human, androgynous personality, there will quite likely be more fully effective and healthy human functioning.

She continues, "An androgynous personality would thus represent the very best of what masculinity and femininity have each come to represent, and the more negative exaggerations of masculinity and femininity would tend to be cancelled out."[5]

Once it becomes clear that we are comfortable with our physical maleness or femaleness, then we go on to ask, do I feel free to experience and express characteristics our culture has said are masculine? that have been considered feminine? Can I put the two characteristics together in a way that is comfortable to me, and that is uniquely me? Bem points out to us that true psychological health may well lie in being able to accomplish this. She therefore goes on to conclude that "the best sex-role identity is no sex-role identity." She urges, "Let sex roles be abolished."[6]

Once we have absorbed Sandra Lipsitz Bem's fairly radical proposal, perhaps then we are set free to ask for ourselves the two basic questions of this whole quest:

1. **What would I like to be rid of?** Of the things that are laid on me because of my culture's assumptions about males, what would I like to give up?

2. **What would I like to appropriate?** Of the things that are denied me because of my culture's assumptions about males, what would I like to have?

Stop, pause, consider those questions. If nothing pops into your mind, give yourself time. The difficulty with which you answer these questions may indicate how strong culture's hold is on you. Or it may indicate you are quite comfortable with traditional masculinity and don't want to let it go.

But as some answers to those questions begin to emerge for me, I feel the need to find a group of men (and perhaps women) with whom I can try out and share these ideas. I may want to try out some behaviors in this safe group, new behaviors that may at first seem strange, awkward or uncomfortable to me. But once the strangeness is past, I will discover what feels right for me. Then I can go out and express these behaviors that feel right for me in society, recognizing where they are denied to me or my sons. And I can set out to influence society to change those points.

Do you remember our discussion of the discovery of women's self awareness as a conversion experience? Females are not the only ones who experience this conversion, for it is at the point of self-discovery that conversion for us males occurs, also. When we become aware of ourselves, we become converted to a freer lifestyle filled with a wider range of possibilities. We become converted to the vision of a world that makes these possibilities available. And we become converted to the attempt to help make the world conform more closely to our own dream.

Part of the freedom we claim in this conversion process is the freedom to be different. We are free to have varying visions of what masculinity means for each of us. I'd like to share my vision of what this free new maleness looks like to me. You, of course, are free to accept or reject what you will out of this vision and to create your own. I conclude by sharing my personal vision with you.

I Am Set Free to Experience Life More Fully

There are so many dimensions of the fuller life in the new role-free masculinity to which I aspire that I will tell you of just some of them. I become less lonely. I shed my competitiveness (well, some of it, little by little), my fear, my suspicion. I overcome my shyness and withdrawal and reach out. Sometimes I feel strange. Sometimes I succeed in my effort, and sometimes I do not. But there is a growing circle of acquaintances, colleagues, friends, and buddies with whom I experience a sense of community. I see more clearly what a precious treasure old friendships that have grown deep truly are, and I become more willing to spend my time and my money to keep in touch with those friends in some way. But I also recognize friendship as a changing, growing, open circle.

I become more open about my emotions. As I become more in touch with what I am feeling, I discover that sometimes I may express it openly and sometimes I may not. But I find myself hungering for those groups and relationships in which I don't have to hide my feelings any more. I become increasingly impatient with the cold, success-oriented settings in which one concentrates only on achievement and ignores experiencing or feeling. This freer expression also is an uncomfortable experience for me at first because I have long repressed angers and rages that are some of the first emotions that appear. But I also have playfulness and humor lurking down there—a childlike mischievousness and joy that somehow I have too seldom acknowledged in my "adult" world.

As I allow myself to experience all the beauty of music, of drama, of people, of relationships, of the gospel—and not to worry whether my emotions are showing or not—the colors in these experiences change from dull grays to magnificent delicate pastels and sometimes brilliant hues.

I become more open about my needs, hopes, expectations and disappointments. I become able to say no. (Well, once in a while; at least I am trying). I communicate more clearly my needs and wants and thus leave experiences with less resentments than I did before.

I become more playful and less competitive. For example, I like to play tennis, but play it very poorly. A person watching my enthusiastic but inept play said to me, "I imagine when you play tennis you are embarrassed a lot." "No," I replied, "I just lose a lot." I could not have said that a few years ago, but I now discover I don't have to be a "loser" just because I lose. We've been outside, we've had fun, we've been together; why should the score matter all that much?

I become less driven and more relaxed. At long stop-lights I can quit being tense and can sit and notice the beautiful yards and the changing seasons; I can take a moment to offer a short prayer (well occasionally, if I'm not too late). At the same time, I intend to work well, to accomplish much and do it well. But I am learning to respond to the needs at hand rather than put on a compulsive frame of reference and keep that same style regardless of what pressures or lack of pressures exist around me.

I leave behind my "Sturdy Oak" image, which requires that I must be the one who knows everything and who is depended on at all times. Instead, I move toward a style of alternation. Sometimes my intimates lean on me, and sometimes I lean on them, and sometimes we lean on each other. But most of the time we each stand on our own, secure in the knowledge that someone is there when he or she is needed.

I am more relaxed about my sexuality. I recognize my homophobia for what it is, a phobia, an illogical fear. I resolve that this fear will not keep me from any interests, friendship, or affection with my male friends. I move in the direction of accepting women as persons. I accept the sexual atmosphere in which I live without overindulging it or feeling as guilty about it as I once did.

I discover freedom to revise my definition of "success." I no longer need numbers, or statistics, or size to prove to me that I have been successful. I no longer have to compete with somebody, beat somebody, be better than somebody to be successful. Success becomes more of an inner harmony with myself, more of sensing a deep relatedness with others. Success occurs for me not so much when I impress others as when I call someone forth. Among my prized possessions is a drawing a friend gave me when I left a previous position. Across the bottom of the drawing, she wrote, "Thank you for taking us with our good, joy, hurts, failures, pain, and indecision and helping us find a bright and strong tomorrow." If her generous gratitude is true in even a small measure, then that is success to me.

Further, I discover a freedom to tolerate and accept ambiguity, vagueness, the unexplainable, the paradox. I do not pretend to understand other religious systems or thought systems or lifestyles, but I do not dismiss them as nonsense just because I do not sense the vitality within them that others do. I do not become excited over the same causes or problems as others, but I sense that they are entitled to pursue "their truth" as I am entitled to search for "my truth." These two truths do not negate or cancel each other out, but are somehow contained in a larger whole than each of us has yet envisioned.

And in all this, life feels richer and fuller to me than it did constrained within society's role expectations for males in our culture.

I Am Set Free to Experience the World of the Spirit

As I become more clearly aware of the impact on me of the masculine role expectations, I make another discovery. In many ways, these same role expectations have blocked, or at least retarded, the development of my faith. These assumptions have stood in the way of my spiritual growth. Consider these examples.

A person starts on the road of spiritual becoming when she or he can say, "I can't make it on my own. Please, God, help me." BUT as a male I have been taught to believe that I am a Sturdy Oak.

A person grows spiritually when one is able to get out of the driver's seat, so to speak, when one is open to being the agency of a power greater than oneself, working through oneself. BUT, the male so often thinks, "I don't want to lose control. I want to be in charge of everything."

A person experiences faith development when that person tells the story of his or her faith pilgrimage to others, examines it, affirms it, and celebrates that God has indeed operated in a life whose story may seem very "ordinary." BUT males have been taught to be tight-lipped, secretive, not to share themselves with others, or not to listen when others share of themselves.

A person grows when, in the words of a church leader of another century, one "attempts great things for God and expects great things from God." That is, one grows when one risks, reaches out, or attempts much more than one thinks she or he can do on her or his own power. When one accomplishes beyond one's own abilities, one senses the divine touch. BUT males have been taught to fear failure and avoid anything that may smack of failure. Thus they are not likely to take risks that may open such doors.

A person grows spiritually when that person is open to the spiritual dimension in all of experience. That is, if a person is open to the divine presence in emotions, thoughts, decisions, actions, then one experiences the realm of the spirit more fully. BUT men are taught to deny their emotions and to be afraid of their emotions. Thus, they have a more difficult time experiencing this beautiful dimension of spiritual becoming. Of course, life in the Spirit is more than emotions alone. Still, it is in the emotions that one sometimes experiences the divine encounter with the greatest clarity. Men are thus apt to be confused or skeptical when people speak of their spiritual awakening.

A person grows spiritually when he or she is open to relationships with other people, both one-on-one and in groups. Other persons may express and communicate to me that divine *koinonia* (fellowship with God). When a person loves me unconditionally, accepts me in spite of my warts and failures, believes in me, touches me, embraces me, encourages me, calls me forth, I experience divine grace. Keith Miller has aptly written, "If you can describe a problem clearly enough, and I have the same problem, suddenly I am no longer alone with my problem, and somehow you have been Christ to me."[7]

A deep trusting relationship with persons may not only have value in itself, but it may be an agency of spiritual growth. BUT males often have difficulty forming trusting relationships because of fear, competitiveness, busyness. And thus we are not likely to experience this dimension of spiritual growth.

A person grows spiritually when one is ready to have one's personality enriched by any gifts of the Spirit or fruit of the Spirit poured out on one. BUT if one responds to such promises as, "But the fruit of the Spirit is love, joy, peace, patience, kindness, goodness, faithfulness, gentleness, self control. . . ." (Galatians 5:22-23) by saying "I'd like just the masculine fruit from that list, please," one is apt to block the flow of any gifts in one's life. Men too often have rigidities built-in that make it difficult to accept and express qualities considered "feminine" in our culture.

I trust that enough of the above examples hit home to you that you see the truth of what I am contending, that cultural role expectations for males have stood in the way of their spiritual becoming and growth.

HOWEVER, as I begin to understand these cultural expectations, question them, resist them, change them, then a wonderful thing happens. I begin to understand faith language and faith possibilities that I only *thought* I understood before. I not only begin to understand them, but I also experiment, claim these spiritual possibilities, and celebrate freely when I experience them.

I am able to say, "I have failed (sinned) and need help." To my great relief I discover that "where sin increased, grace abounded all the more" (Romans 5:20).

I make beginning attempts to be open to powers greater than myself, to give up control, and I discover that "when I am weak then I am strong" (2 Corinthians 12:10b).

I timidly experiment with telling pieces of my faith story, and I listen to others and am touched by the power of their stories and mine.

In my storytelling and hearing, I open myself to others more than I have before. And I discover that it is indeed true; in the acceptance, sharing, and joy of other people, I am graced by the presence and love of God.

I try some new things in service of my faith, expecting to look foolish, be ridiculed, and fail. I don't always succeed, but sometimes

I do, aware that the accomplishment came through an empowerment of my life. And when I fail, it matters less, for I have learned to pray with Peter Marshall that God will help me to know that it is better to fail in causes that will ultimately succeed than to succeed in causes that will ultimately fail.

I try being open to all the emotions that touch my life. In the faith at first it is difficult, but as I laugh and cry, celebrate and sorrow, sense isolation and presence, I become still and know that God is God.

As I sense God's new (to me) gifts touching me, I begin to discover (not just vaguely affirm in some remote corner of my head) that "there is neither male nor female; for (we) are all one in Christ Jesus" (Galatians 3:28).

I am set free to grow spiritually, to be in a process of spiritual becoming. Exciting possibilities beckon to me now, and beyond these immediate possibilities, there are infinitely more over the horizon of my present imagination. I think I'm experiencing something akin to what Paul meant when he spoke of "the glorious liberty of the children of God" (Romans 8:21).

I Am Set Free for Others

George Romney, Edmund Muskie, Thomas Eagleton—what do these three men have in common, besides being politicians?

Each of them experienced a severely damaged political career because of an admission of weakness. George Romney admitted that he had been "brainwashed" about the Vietnam war and that he had changed his mind about it. Public reaction did not reward a man big enough to learn from his mistakes and go on from there. Rather, the press and public opinion leveled such a barrage of criticism against him that eventually Romney withdrew from the primary race and yielded to a man less willing to admit vulnerability, Richard Nixon.

In the next presidential campaign, Edmund Muskie, while countering a slur on his wife, broke into tears. Press and public response was *not* "Here is a sensitive man who cares deeply about his family." Rather, the reaction was that he revealed himself to be ". . . a man who tires easily and tends toward emotional outbursts under pressure."[8]

And in the next presidential campaign, Thomas Eagleton was forced to resign his vice presidential candidacy because he admitted that he had had treatment for depression, including electric shock treatments, the last of which occured six years before his candidacy. In those six years there was no indication of recurrence of the problem for which he had sought and received help. The admission that he was vulnerable and that he had obtained help indicted him and cost him his candidacy.[9]

What do John F. Kennedy, Lyndon Johnson, and Richard Nixon have in common—besides all being former presidents of our nation?

In the opinion of some sensitive political observers, all three of them allowed the "Sturdy Oak" image, the manly air of toughness, confidence, and self-reliance to be a key factor in their policies about Vietnam. Marc Feigen Fasteau speaks of "the cult of toughness" in foreign policy. He asks why we persisted in a hopeless war beyond the time when there was any reasonable hope of its being meaningful. After careful study and analysis, he concludes that at least part of this answer was the need to be "tough." [10]

John Kennedy told journalist James Reston of his thoughts after an unsettling meeting with Kruschev.

> I've got a terrible problem. If he thinks I'm inexperienced and have no guts, until we remove those ideas, we won't get anywhere with him. So we have to act. . . . Now we have a problem in trying to make our power credible, and Vietnam looks like the place. [11]

And so he sent military advisors and support teams to Vietnam. Their numbers grew to fifteen thousand by the end of his presidency.

Fasteau notes this theme of toughness continued in Johnson's presidency. He quotes journalist David Halberstam in this analysis:

> He (Johnson) had always been haunted by the idea that he would be judged as being insufficiently manly for the job, that he would lack courage at a crucial moment. More than a little insecure himself, he wanted very much to be seen as a man; it was a conscious thing. . . . He wanted the respect of men who were tough, real men, and they would turn out to be hawks. . . . [12]

And so the escalation and the bombing continued, a result of these masculine fears, at least in part.

Johnson was succeeded by Richard Nixon, who proclaimed, "We will not be humiliated. It is not our power but our will and character that is being tested. . . ." He pledged that he would not let the United States become "a second-rate power" and "accept the first defeat in its proud one-hundred-ninety-year history." [13]

Brannon and David summarize this tragic episode of foreign policy history with these words, "Thousands of American men lie dead in Vietnam, and the male sex role may well have been the largest single factor in determining why they were ordered to go." [14]

Sadly, we cannot consider this a historical period of madness from which we learned and which we have left behind. The trend continues. A recent news analysis article examining our government's military involvement in Central America carries this summary title "U.S.

'Macho' Quest May Lead to a Genocidal War''[15] This title is a summary that many observers feel is all too accurate. Eugene Bianchi has observed, "Deliberation and decision at the top take place in a male lodge where the cultural myths of masculinity reign supreme."[16]

Think about this for a minute: in a world with limited and shrinking resources, an extremely tight economy, and innumerable tragic human needs, nations are unable to respond to these needs while they continue to spend more than they want to for armies, defenses, and weapons that can overkill their opposition several times over! Does that make any sense?

What gains there will be when at least we can discuss and explore these issues freely, when we can search for a better way! Somehow we need to kick "The Sturdy Oak," "The Big Wheel," the "No Sissy Stuff," and the "Give 'em Hell" out of the State Department, the Pentagon, the White House and all other levels of government as well. We must believe that there can be another way, and then we must choose and support leaders who will explore alternatives.

Discovering that unexamined traditional male roles were impacting on crucial foreign policy decisions was an eye opener to me. It caused me to ask two other questions: Who else is affected by our culture's assumptions about males? Who else am *I* affecting when I unthinkingly express my culture's assumptions about maleness? As I live with these questions, I discover the answers are more vast and far reaching than I had previously imagined.

Elizabeth Dodson Gray, for example, has shown how male roles and attitudes have created a distance, a competition, a struggle, with *nature* and the *whole ecosystem* itself. She writes,

> It is important for us to see that men have done with Mother Nature this same dominance/submission flip-flop. They have by their technologies worked steadily and for generations to transform a psychologically intolerable dependence upon a seemingly powerful and capricious "Mother Nature" into a soothing and acceptable dependence upon a subservient and non-threatening "wife." This "need to be above" and to dominate permeates male attitudes toward nature. It is as though men did not like *any* feelings of depending upon "Mother Nature." Nature must be below, just as Wife must be below, for to be a man, *a man must be in control!*[17]

Gray holds forth a vision of harmonious participation for human beings in the whole created order. This vision arises out of her reflection upon her experience as a woman in dialogue with the vision of men. She then asks,

> But the question now is whether we—especially males—can accept the giver of new symbols, new metaphors, and new modes of viewing reality

if the giver is Woman. Can the male give up his old monopoly on the role of decisive gift-giver? Can he share with Woman the role of image-maker in the culture? Even beyond that, can Man find in himself the open hand to receive a new image to complement his own when the giver is The Other? Even if his life depends on it?[18]

The argument thus far is that male role attitudes permeate the way our nations arm against each other and contend with each other, and that these same attitudes invade our basic view of the whole of nature. These attitudes have brought us into dangerous conflict with the powerful forces of nature. Survival and quality of life for all living things are some of the benefits that can come when the traditional male role begins to change and when these changes are expressed in changed ways of relating and doing things. But there are more immediate gains for others as well.

My claiming of a new male style of life can have important effect where I work. We co-workers can change from a body of competitors to a community of colleagues. We can change our place of work from a place where one hides pains, struggles, and feelings, to an environment where there is understanding, interest, permission to speak about such matters. We can change from an attitude of everyone for him or herself to one of giving and receiving support, consultation, and advice. I can begin to change my place of work by allowing myself to change and inviting others into that changing work relationship.

I can help change some of the loneliness I sense in myself and in those all around me. I can make an effort to leave behind that pseudo-friendship. I can reach out to a few others with more transparency, trust, and invitation to deeper intimacy.

If I am married, and if I am a parent, I can better serve my family by role-free husbanding and parenting. I begin to change my perception about the household tasks from "hers" and "his" to "ours," selected on the basis of skill, interest, need, and time. I relate more transparently to both my wife and my children. I become much more clearly aware that whatever the sex of my children, each child should have opportunity to shake off old sex-role expectations, to experience, discover, explore, and become all that she or he wants to be. I can be less angry and dominating and more sharing and joyful in my relationship with my children.

I can have an impact upon the life of my church as well. I can create a freer and more flexible environment by volunteering for tasks in which I have an interest, but which were previously assigned to women only. Similarly, I can nominate women for places of leadership once reserved for men alone (these are probably places of power and prestige). When my church calls a pastor, I can remind those selecting the pastor to give consideration to all qualified candidates, regardless of age, sex, or ethnicity. I can express openness and enthusiasm for worship language, Bible translations, and images that use female as well as male metaphors about God. Perhaps my enthusiasm and openness can help others feel a little more free to consider such changes.

I can do all these things without having to persuade everyone to be just like me. I don't have to compete with those who disagree. I don't have to dominate those who do not share my viewpoint. I don't have to be in control. I don't have to "win." I can simply give my witness, be sure that it is listened to, and trust the process that whatever truth there is in it will someday be heard and accepted.

Brothers and sisters, our conversion continues. The first turnings in this conversion were painful to be sure. But what felt like pain now begins to feel like promise!

Appendix

The Church's Task in Helping Men and Women Deal with Their Changing Roles

While my focus has been on helping the male become conscious of and make changes in his role expectations, I'd like to share a brief word in conclusion about the church's task in helping both men and women deal with this issue.

Some "What" Propositions

I believe that human liberation is a basic aspect of the gospel. Indeed liberation is the gospel itself! Thus, it deserves attention within the church community. I believe also that compassion for persons who are hurt by liberation's uneven progress mandates that the church give more attention to this subject than it has given in the past.

I believe that men's and women's liberation issues are integrally related to such issues as militarism and war, hunger and starvation, family stability, and person abuse. The human liberation movement should always be explored in full view of some of these great issues to which it is interrelated.

I believe that even when men are not aware of the issues involving men's role stereotypes, they still have a hunger and need to learn to trust, to relate, to make friends, to get in touch with their feelings, to reach out and care. Support groups that can gently lead men in this direction are both wanted and needed.

I believe that, particularly within the church, neither men nor women should discuss roles and liberation issues in isolation from each other. Men should not consider them in isolation from the women nor women in isolation from the men. However, each group may need a considerable amount of time before they are ready to discuss them with the other. Likewise, I believe that if a church is going to have a group for men on these issues, it should have one for women, and vice versa. While these groups may need to be all men or all women for a time, they also need to share with each other what they are discovering, and, if necessary, hold each other accountable for what they are concluding.

I believe that although it may be necessary for men and women to meet separately from each other so that they may explore feelings, share secrets, experience distance, and express anger that comes from having participated in an oppressive system, the ultimate goal should be reconciliation with each other through the One in whom there is neither male nor female. Theologian Nelle Morton has said, "Any theology developed by one sex, out of the experience of one sex, cannot be lived out as if it were a whole theology." [1] That is what we have been doing for too long. By telling, hearing, and exploring in depth with eyes of faith the experiences of each sex, perhaps we can begin to develop that whole theology for a whole person.

Some "How" Propositions

If you agree that dialogue about sex roles is a need, where do you find the group to work on these topics? Some begin with an existing group—an ongoing church school class, women's circle, or men's group. One pastor told me that one year his men's group, which met for a monthly dinner meeting, was sitting around after supper each month telling jokes and trying to figure out interesting programs. The next year it was eagerly reading books on men's roles, and the next year it spent its time creating new rituals for ways men could relate to each other supportively.

More frequently (and usually better) a group should be called together for this specific purpose. I say this is usually better because no one should be railroaded into discussing these topics against his or her will. One should not worry if the group wanting to deal with these matters is very small. That may be better. I attempted to lead a support group of fifteen to eighteen men, and that was too large. We had to spend lots of our time in sub-groups of three or four persons to develop the comfort and trust needed to explore the sensitive issues we discussed.

Once you get the group together, then what? Here are some possible content suggestions:

An all men's group (or possibly one that included women) might want to discuss Herb Goldberg's significant books, *The Hazards of Being Male* (New York: New American Library, 1976), and *The New Male* (New York: New American Library, 1979). I would not hesitate to use these books (thoroughly previewed) with a group that really wanted to explore feelings and experiences. However, someone should be ready to examine assumptions and Christian perspectives on the themes Goldberg explores. I personally find him to be a fascinating, compassionate, insightful writer, but I part company with him often out of concern that I operate within my faith perspective.

A group of men, women, or both might want to discuss Virginia Ramey Mollenkott's, *Women, Men, and the Bible* (Nashville: Abingdon, 1977). There is a study kit with this book which includes a guide, cassettes narrated by the author, and all that is needed for a twelve-hour study course. This might well be where many persons need to begin if they are to gain freedom as people of the Bible to explore male/female role issues as freely as I have done in the preceding pages.

If a group would like to dialogue about liberation issues from a woman's and from a man's perspective, it might be useful to study two books in parallel fashion. I would suggest using Letha Scanzoni and Nancy Hardesty's *All We're Meant to Be* (Waco, Tex.: Word, Inc., 1974) and this book, *Changing Male Roles in Today's World*, simultaneously. It would not be at all difficult to match chapters on many subjects so that one could explore these common themes from a Christian woman's and a Christian man's perspective.

If a group would prefer to be less a "study group" and more one that reflects and learns from contemporary experiences, I suggest three resources to help you establish such a group.

1. Clarke G. Carney and Sarah Lynne McMahon, *Exploring Contemporary Male/Female Roles: A Facilitator's Guide* (San Diego: University Associates, Inc., 1977). This book contains twenty-four structured exercises that allow a group to discover something about their own sex-role attitudes and then gives opportunities to discuss and reflect upon what they have discovered. Readings on the subject are also included.

2. Charlotte Holt Clinebell, *Counseling for Liberation* (Philadelphia: Fortress Press, 1976). In addition to discussing the issues of human liberation, Clinebell's chapter 6 offers useful "Techniques for Counseling and Consciousness Raising."

3. Warren Farrell, *The Liberated Man* (New York: Random House, Inc., 1974). The final section of this book includes three especially pertinent chapters: one on men's consciousness-raising groups, one on joint consciousness-raising groups (which he says is where the future lies), and one providing additional topics and techniques in running consciousness-raising groups.

The books I have listed here are the ones from which I have learned much as I pursued this project. I hope you find them helpful as well.

But whatever the resources and style you select, I cannot emphasize too strongly my conviction that the church needs to provide opportunity and support for persons concerned about these issues. By entering into this process, the church may know the joy of being of help to some of the most energetic, sensitive, creative, perceptive, and hurting of all God's people.

Notes

Chapter 1
The Way It Was

[1] Deborah S. David and Robert Brannon, eds., *The Forty-Nine Percent Majority: The Male Sex Role* (Reading, Mass.: Addison-Wesley Publishing Co., Inc., 1976), p. 5. Reprinted with permission.

[2] *Ibid.*, p. 1.

[3] Margaret Mead, *Sex and Temperament in Three Primitive Societies* (New York: Dell Publishing Co., Inc., 1968. First published in 1935 by William Morrow and Co., Inc.).

[4] *Ibid.*, p. 213.

[5] *Ibid.*, p. 241.

[6] *Ibid.*, p. 260.

[7] Letha Scanzoni and Nancy Hardesty, *All We're Meant to Be* (Waco, Tex.: Word, Inc., 1974), p. 77.

[8] Virginia Ramey Mollenkott, *Women, Men, and the Bible* (Nashville: Abingdon Press, 1977), pp. 77-78.

[9] Warren Farrell, *The Liberated Man* (New York: Random House, Inc., 1974), p. 172.

[10] Mollenkott, *op. cit.*, p. 78.

[11] Reprinted from Peter N. Stearns, *Be a Man!* (New York: Holmes & Meier Publishers, Inc., 1979), p. 2. Copyright © 1979 by Peter N. Stearns. Used by permission.

[12] *Ibid.*, p. 3.

[13] *Ibid.*

[14] *Ibid.*, p. 16.

[15] *Ibid.*, p. 22.

[16] *Ibid.*

[17] *Ibid.*, p. 31.

[18] *Ibid.*, p. 45.

[19] *Ibid.*, p. 49.

[20] *Ibid.*, p. 62.

[21] *Ibid.*, p. 63.

[22] *Ibid.*, p. 71.

23 *Ibid.*, p. 76.
24 *Ibid.*, p. 83.

Chapter 2
The Way It Is

1 James E. Kilgore, *Being a Man in a Woman's World* (Irvine, Calif.: Harvest House Publishers, 1975), p. 26. Used by permission of the author.
2 *Ibid.*, pp. 26-27.
3 Deborah S. David and Robert Brannon, eds., *The Forty-Nine Percent Majority: The Male Sex Role* (Reading, Mass.: Addison-Wesley Publishing Co., Inc., 1976). Reprinted with permission.
4 *Ibid.*, pp. 13-19.
5 *Ibid.*, p. 19.
6 *Ibid.*, p. 23.
7 *Ibid.*, p. 25.
8 *Ibid.*, pp. 26-27.
9 *Ibid.*, p. 27.
10 *Ibid.*
11 *Ibid.*, pp. 34-35.
12 *Ibid.*, p. 31.
13 *Ibid.*, p. 32.
14 *Ibid.*, pp. 35-36.
15 Warren Farrell, *The Liberated Man* (New York: Random House, Inc., 1974), p. 32.
16 Ann Wilson Schaef, *Women's Reality, An Emerging Female System in the White Male Society* (Minneapolis: Winston Press, Inc., 1981), p. 2. Copyright © 1981 by Anne Wilson Schaef. Published by Winston Press, Inc., 430 Oak Grove, Minneapolis, MN 55403. All rights reserved. Used by permission.
17 *Ibid.*, p. 8.
18 *Ibid.*, p. 9.
19 *Ibid.*, p. 10.
20 *Ibid.*, p. 15.
21 *Ibid.*
22 *Ibid.*
23 *Ibid.*, p. 16.
24 Herb Goldberg, *The Hazards of Being Male: Surviving the Myth of Masculine Privilege* (New York: The New American Library, Inc., 1976), p. 5.
25 James C. Dobson, *Straight Talk to Men and Their Wives* (Waco, Tex.: Word, Inc., 1980), pp. 156-157.
26 *Ibid.*, p. 157.

Chapter 3
On the Way to What Will Be

1 Virginia Ramey Mollenkott, *Women, Men, and the Bible* (Nashville: Abingdon Press, 1977), p. 91.
2 *Ibid.*, pp. 10-11.
3 William Barclay, *The Letter to the Hebrews* (Edinburgh: The Saint Andrew Press, 1955), pp. 18-19.
4 Mollenkott, *op. cit.*, p. 74.
5 *Ibid.*, p. 132.
6 *Ibid.*
7 Letha Scanzoni and Nancy Hardesty, *All We're Meant to Be* (Waco, Tex.: Word, Inc., 1974), p. 59. Copyright © 1974, 1975. Used by permission Word Books, Publisher, Waco, TX 76796.
8 Mollenkott, *op. cit.*, p. 85.
9 Scanzoni and Hardesty, *op. cit.*, p. 87.
10 Deborah S. David and Robert Brannon, eds., *The Forty-Nine Percent Majority: The*

Male Sex Role (Reading, Mass.: Addison-Wesley Publishing Co., Inc., 1976), p. 12. Reprinted with permission.

[11] Shusaku Endo, *A Life of Jesus* (New York: Paulist Press, 1978), p. 51.
[12] David and Brannon, *op. cit.,* p. 12.
[13] *Ibid.*
[14] *Ibid.*

Chapter 4
Claiming the Freedom to Feel

[1] Herb Goldberg, Ph.D., *The Hazards of Being Male: Surviving the Myth of Masculine Privilege* (New York: The New American Library, Inc., 1976).
[2] *Ibid.,* p. 45.
[3] *Ibid.,* p. 46.
[4] *Ibid.*
[5] Herb Goldberg, *The New Male from Self-Destruction to Self-Care* (New York: The New American Library, Inc., 1979), pp. 13-14.
[6] Goldberg, *Hazards,* p. 48.
[7] *Ibid.*
[8] Warren Farrell, *The Liberated Man* (New York: Random House, Inc., 1974), pp. 72-73.
[9] Goldberg, *Hazards,* pp. 49-50.
[10] Farrell, *op. cit.,* pp. 71-72.
[11] Phyllis Chesler, *About Men* (New York: Simon and Schuster, Inc., 1978), p. 142. Copyright © 1978 by Phyllis Chesler. Reprinted by permission of Simon & Schuster, a division of Gulf & Western Corporation.
[12] Sidney M. Jourard, *The Transparent Self: Self-Disclosure and Well-Being* (New York: D. Van Nostrand Co., 1964), pp. 46-55.
[13] Goldberg, *Hazards,* pp. 48-49.
[14] Goldberg, *The New Male,* p. 51.
[15] *Ibid.,* pp. 52-53.
[16] Goldberg, *Hazards,* p. 50.
[17] *Ibid.,* p. 51.
[18] *Ibid.,* p. 55.
[19] *Ibid.*
[20] Farrell, *op. cit.,* pp. 328-329.
[21] Goldberg, *Hazards,* pp. 58-59.
[22] *Ibid.,* p. 59.

Chapter 5
Charting the Wilderness

[1] Shere Hite, *The Hite Report on Male Sexuality* (New York: Alfred A. Knopf, Inc., 1981) as quoted by Lynn Langway in "Now, the Trouble with Men," *Newsweek,* June 15, 1981, pp. 104-107.
[2] Vance Packard, *The Sexual Wilderness* (New York: Pocket Books, 1970; originally published by David McKay Co., Inc., 1968).
[3] *Ibid.,* pp. 69-70. Packard stated indebtedness to Isadore Rubin for this classification of existing sexual value systems.
[4] Lynn Langway, "Now, the Trouble with Men," *Newsweek,* June 15, 1981, p. 104.
[5] Gregory K. Lehne, "Homophobia Among Men," in *The Forty-Nine Percent Majority: The Male Sex Role,* ed. Deborah S. David and Robert Brannon (Reading, Mass.: Addison-Wesley Publishing Co., Inc., 1976), p. 66.
[6] *Ibid.,* pp. 66-85.
[7] Herb Goldberg, *The New Male from Self-Destruction to Self-Care* (New York: The New American Library, Inc., 1979), p. 95.
[8] Langway, *op. cit., Newsweek,* p. 104.
[9] Emert H. Dose, "So, Mr. Macho, What's More Important Than Sex?" *Racine Journal Times,* 1980.

Chapter 6
Breaking Through the Relationship Barrier

[1] Herb Goldberg, *The New Male from Self-Destruction to Self-Care* (New York: The New American Library, Inc., 1979), p. 9.

[2] Daniel J. Levinson *et al.*, *The Seasons of a Man's Life* (New York: Alfred A. Knopf, Inc., 1978), p. 335.

[3] Phyllis Chesler, *About Men* (New York: Simon and Schuster, Inc., 1978) p. 234. Copyright © 1978 by Phyllis Chesler. Reprinted by permission of Simon & Schuster a division of Gulf & Western Corporation.

[4] *Ibid.*, p. 236.

[5] *Ibid.*, pp. 239-240.

[6] *Ibid.*, p. 240.

[7] *Ibid.*, p. 241.

[8] *Ibid.*, pp. 243-244.

[9] Herb Goldberg, *The Hazards of Being Male: Surviving the Myth of Masculine Privilege* (New York: The New American Library, Inc., 1976), p. 132.

[10] Joel D. Block, *Friendship* (New York: Macmillan, Inc., 1980), p. 55. Copyright © 1980 by Joel D. Block.

[11] *Ibid.*, pp. 13-14.

[12] *Ibid.*, p. 14.

[13] Goldberg, *Hazards*, p. 128.

[14] Block, *op. cit.*, pp. 71-72.

[15] Deborah S. David and Robert Brannon, eds., *The Forty-Nine Percent Majority: The Male Sex Role* (Reading, Mass.: Addison-Wesley Publishing Co., Inc., 1976), p. 18. Reprinted with permission.

[16] Goldberg, *Hazards*, p. 135.

[17] *Ibid.*

[18] *Ibid.*, pp. 136-137.

Chapter 7
Finding Help from an Unexpected Source

[1] Joyce McCarl Nielsen, *Sex in Society, Perspectives on Stratification* (Belmont, Calif.: Wadsworth, Inc., 1978), p. 150.

[2] *Ibid.*, pp. 150-151.

[3] Letha Scanzoni and Nancy Hardesty, *All We're Meant to Be* (Waco, Tex.: Word, Inc., 1974), p. 11.

[4] *Ibid.*, p. 207.

[5] Herb Goldberg, *The New Male from Self-Destruction to Self-Care* (New York: The New American Library, Inc., 1979), p. 141.

[6] *Ibid.*, pp. 142-143.

[7] *Ibid.*, p. 7.

[8] *Ibid.*, p. 181.

[9] *Ibid.*, p. 185.

[10] Warren Farrell, *The Liberated Man* (New York: Random House, Inc., 1974), chapter 10, pp. 175-191. I acknowledge my indebtedness to Mr. Farrell for most of the suggestions of possible gains for men.

[11] Goldberg, *op. cit.*, pp. 189-190.

Chapter 8
Not Robert, or Dagwood, but You

[1] James A. Levine, *Who Will Raise the Children?* (Philadelphia: J. P. Lippincott Co., 1976), p. 21.

[2] Mary C. Howell, "Employed Mothers and Their Families," *Pediatrics*, vol. 52, no. 2 (August, 1973), p. 7, as quoted in *ibid.*, p. 27.

[3] Levine, *op. cit.*, p. 30.

[4]Martin Greenberg, M.D., and Norman Morris, M.D., "Engrossment: The Newborn's Impact upon the Father," *American Journal of Orthopsychiatry*, vol. 44, no. 4 (July, 1974), pp. 522-528, as quoted in Levine, *op. cit.*, p. 30.

[5]Levine, *op. cit.*, pp. 101-102.

[6]James C. Dobson, *What Wives Wish Their Husbands Knew About Women* (Wheaton, Ill.: Tyndale House Publishers, 1975), p. 158.

[7]Ruth E. Hartley, "Sex-Role Pressures and the Socialization of the Male Child," in *The Forty-Nine Percent Majority: The Male Sex Role* ed. Deborah S. David and Robert Brannon (Reading, Mass.: Addison-Wesley Publishing Co., Inc., 1976), p. 237.

[8]Levine, *op. cit.*, pp. 152-153.

[9]*Ibid.*, pp. 71-72.

[10]*Ibid.*, pp. 76-83.

[11]*Ibid.*, pp. 127-132.

[12]Letty Cottin Pogrebin, *Growing Up Free: Raising Your Child in the 80's* (New York: McGraw-Hill, Inc., 1980).

[13]*Ibid.*, pp. 55-72. Used with the permission of McGraw-Hill Book Company.

[14]James C. Dobson, *Dare to Discipline* (Wheaton, Ill.: Tyndale House Publishers, 1970).

Chapter 9
You Don't Own Her Anymore

[1]Letha and John Scanzoni, *Men, Women, and Change* (New York: McGraw-Hill, Inc., 1976), pp. 245, 214, as noted by Virginia Ramey Mollenkott in *Women, Men, and the Bible* (Nashville: Abingdon Press, 1977), pp. 37-38.

[2]Mollenkott, *op. cit.*, p. 41.

[3]*Ibid.*, p. 23.

[4]*Ibid.*, p. 27.

[5]*Ibid.*, p. 137.

[6]Caroline Bird, *The Two-Paycheck Marriage* (New York: Pocket Books, 1979), p. 3.

[7]*Ibid.*, pp. 30-40.

[8]G. Wade Rowatt, Jr., and Mary Jo Brock Rowatt, *The Two-Career Marriage* (Philadelphia: The Westminster Press, 1980). Used by permission.

[9]*Ibid.*, p. 13.

[10]*Ibid.*, p. 14.

[11]*Ibid.*, p. 15.

[12]*Ibid.*

[13]*Ibid.*, pp. 13-19.

[14]*Ibid.*, pp. 26-40.

[15]Francine S. and Douglas T. Hall, *The Two-Career Couple* (Reading, Mass.: Addison-Wesley Publishing Co., Inc., 1979), pp. 51-53. Reprinted from *The Two-Career Couple* by Francine and Douglas T. Hall, Copyright © 1979, by permission of Addison-Wesley Publishing Co., Reading, MA.

[16]*Ibid.*, p. 166.

[17]Warren Farrell, "The Politics of Vulnerability," in *The Forty-Nine Percent Majority: The Male Sex Role,* ed. Deborah S. David and Robert Brannon (Reading, Mass.: Addison-Wesley Publishing Co., Inc., 1976), p. 54.

[18]Darrell Sifford, "Some Husbands Aren't Threatened by Wife's Success," *Boulder Daily Camera,* June 2, 1981, p. 5.

Chapter 10
Competitors, Colleagues, Bosses

[1]*Input,* published by the Division of Communications, American Baptist Churches, USA, vol. 11, no. 24 (December 4, 1980), p. 3.

[2]Peter N. Stearns, *Be a Man!* (New York: Holmes & Meier Publishers, Inc., 1979), p. 118.

[3]Marilyn Brown Oden, *Beyond Feminism* (Nashville: Abingdon Press, 1971), p. 35.

[4] "Publicity Forces Bendix Executive to Leave Position," *Boulder Daily Camera* (October 9, 1980), p. 10.

[5] Barbara Benedict Bunker and Edith Whitfield Seashore, "Power, Collusion, Intimacy-Sexuality, Support: Breaking the Sex-Role Stereotypes in Social and Organizational Settings," in *Exploring Contemporary Male/Female Roles: A Facilitator's Guide,* ed. Clarke G. Carney and Sarah Lynne McMahon (San Diego: University Associates, Inc., 1977), p. 252.

[6] James E. Kilgore, *Being a Man in a Woman's World* (Irvine, Calif.: Harvest House Publishers, 1975), pp. 98-99. Used by permission of the author.

Chapter 11
The Tender Mercies of the God Who Bore Us

[1] Letha Scanzoni and Nancy Hardesty, *All We're Meant to Be* (Waco Tex.: Word, Inc., 1974), p. 20. Copyright © 1974, 1975. Used by permission Word Books, Publishers, Waco, TX, 76796.

[2] Mary Ann Tolbert, "The Bible and Sexist Language," in *Language About God in Liturgy and Scripture: A Study Guide* (Philadelphia: The Geneva Press, 1980), p. 17.

[3] Virginia Ramey Mollenkott, *Women, Men and the Bible* (Nashville: Abingdon Press, 1977), p. 58.

[4] Phyllis Trible, *God and the Rhetoric of Sexuality* (Philadelphia: Fortress Press, 1978), pp. 31-49, as cited by Mary Ann Tolbert in "The Bible and Sexist Language," from *Language About God in Liturgy and Scripture: A Study Guide* (Philadelphia: The Geneva Press, 1980), p. 18.

[5] Minutes of the 120th General Assembly of the Presbyterian Church in the United States (Southern), May 30–June 6, 1980, Myrtle Beach, S.C. p. 281.

[6] Kenneth Woodward and Don Kirk, "Finding Jesus in Japan," *Newsweek,* December 1, 1980, p. 106.

[7] Shusaku Endo, *A Life of Jesus* (New York: Paulist Press, 1978), p. 1.

[8] Woodward and Kirk, *op. cit.,* p. 106.

[9] Krister Stendahl, "Enrichment or Treat? When the Eves Come Marching In," from *Sexist Religion and Women in the Church: No More Silence,* ed. Alice Hageman (Wilton, Conn.: Association Press, 1974), as quoted by Linda J. Clark, "In Christ There Is No East or West," in *Language About God in Liturgy and Scripture: A Study Guide* (Philadelphia: The Geneva Press, 1980), p. 29.

[10] "The NCC and Inclusive Biblical Language," in *Feminism and the Church Today Fact Sheet,* published by National Ministries, American Baptist Churches, U.S.A., vol. 5, no. 1 (March, 1981), p. 9.

[11] Don Postema, "Do I Belong?" *Daughters of Sarah,* vol. 5, no. 2 (March/April, 1979), pp. 14-15.

[12] Ann Patrick Ware, "Some Implications of the Feminist Movement for the Church," *Living Ecumenism Series,* series 5, no. 1 (March, 1980), pp. 18-19.

[13] Linda J. Clark, "In Christ There Is No East or West," in *Language About God in Liturgy and Scripture: A Study Guide* (Philadelphia: The Geneva Press, 1980), p. 26. Used by permission.

[14] *Ibid.,* pp. 27-28.

[15] Ware, *op. cit.,* p. 21.

Chapter 12
The Tender Mercies (continued)

[1] Edward C. Lehman, Jr., and the Task Force on Women in Ministry of the Ministers Council, *Project S.W.I.M., A Study of Women in Ministry* (Valley Forge: American Baptist Churches, U.S.A., n.d.), p. ii.

[2] Letha Scanzoni and Nancy Hardesty, *All We're Meant to Be* (Waco, Tex.: Word, Inc., 1974), p. 68.

[3] *Ibid.,* pp. 70-71.

[4] Elizabeth Florenza, "Women in the Early Christian Movement," in *Womanspirit*

Rising, ed. Carol Christ and Judith Plaskow (San Francisco: Harper & Row, Publishers, Inc., 1979), p. 88.

[5]*Ibid.*

[6]Scanzoni and Hardesty, *op. cit.,* p. 62.

[7]Florenza, *op. cit.,* p. 90.

[8]"Forgotten Women: Female Priests of the Early Church," in *Feminism and the Church Today Fact Sheet,* published by National Ministries, American Baptist Churches, U.S.A., vol. 5, no. 1 (March 1981), p. 13. The article cited was from *The Witness.*

[9]Virginia Ramey Mollenkott, *Women, Men, and the Bible* (Nashville: Abingdon Press, 1977), p. 104.

[10]Calvin J. Roetzel, *The Letters of Paul: Conversations in Context* (Atlanta: John Knox, 1975), p. 101, quoted in Mollenkott, *op. cit.,* p. 105.

[11]Mollenkott, *op. cit.,* p. 106.

[12]Scanzoni and Hardesty, *op. cit.,* p. 178.

[13]Carol Christ and Marilyn Collins, "Shattering the Idols of Men: Theology from the Perspective of Women's Experience," *Reflection,* vol. 69 (May 1972), published by Yale Divinity School, p. 12.

Chapter 13
A New Vision, a New Freedom

[1]Charlotte Holt Clinebell, *Counseling for Liberation* (Philadelphia: Fortress Press, 1976), p. 20.

[2]*Ibid.*

[3]Sandra Lipsitz Bem, "Beyond Androgyny: Some Presumptous Prescriptions for a Liberated Sexual Identity," in *Exploring Contemporary Male/Female Roles: A Facilitator's Guide,* ed. Clarke G. Carney and Sarah Lynne McMahon (San Diego: University Associates, 1977), p. 227.

[4]*Ibid.,* p. 213.

[5]*Ibid.*

[6]*Ibid.,* pp. 226-227.

[7]Keith Miller, *Faith at Work,* February, 1974, cover.

[8]Warren Farrell, "The Politics of Vulnerability," in *The Forty-Nine Percent Majority: The Male Sex Role,* ed. Deborah S. David and Robert Brannon (Reading, Mass.: Addison-Wesley Publishing Co., Inc., 1976), pp. 51-52. He is quoting from *The New York Times,* March 9, 1972, p. 32.

[9]Farrell, *op. cit.,* p. 52.

[10]Marc Feigen Fasteau, "Vietnam and the Cult of Toughness in Foreign Policy," from *The Male Machine* (New York: McGraw-Hill, Inc., 1974), in *The Forty-Nine Percent Majority,* ed. David and Brannon, *op. cit.,* pp. 158-189.

[11]David Halberstam, *The Best and the Brightest* (New York: Random House, Inc., 1972), p. 76.

[12]*Ibid.,* p. 531.

[13]Lucy Komisar, "Violence and the Masculine Mystique," in *The Forty-Nine Percent Majority,* ed. David and Brannon, *op. cit.,* p. 201.

[14]Deborah S. David and Robert Brannon, eds., *The Forty-Nine Percent Majority: The Male Sex Role* (Reading, Mass.: Addison-Wesley Publishing Co. Inc., 1976), p. 183.

[15]Lucy Komisar, *Denver Post* (March 8, 1981).

[16]Elizabeth Dodson Gray, *Green Paradise Lost,* originally *Why the Green Nigger? Remything Genesis* (Wellesley, Mass.: Roundtable Press, 1979), p. 39.

[17]*Ibid.,* p. 42.

[18]*Ibid.,* p. 117.

Appendix

[1]Nelle Morton, "Toward a Whole Theology" (address delivered at World Council of Churches Task Force on Women), as quoted in *Counseling for Liberation* by Charlotte Holt Clinebell (Philadelphia: Fortress Press, 1976), p. 59.